RICHARD M JONES

Lockington
CRASH AT THE
CROSSING

RICHARD M JONES

Lockington
CRASH AT THE
CROSSING

MEREO

Cirencester

Mereo Books

1A The Wool Market Dyer Street Cirencester Gloucestershire GL7 2PR
An imprint of Memoirs Publishing www.mereobooks.com

Lockington- Crash at the Crossing: 978-1-86151-229-1

First published in Great Britain in 2014
by Mereo Books, an imprint of Memoirs Publishing

The address for Memoirs Publishing Group Limited can be found at
www.memoirspublishing.com

The Memoirs Publishing Group Ltd Reg. No. 7834348

The Memoirs Publishing Group supports both The Forest Stewardship Council® (FSC®)
and the PEFC® leading international forest-certification organisations. Our books carrying
both the FSC label and the PEFC® and are printed on FSC®-certified paper. FSC® is the only
forest-certification scheme supported by the leading environmental organisations including
Greenpeace. Our paper procurement policy can be found at
www.memoirspublishing.com/environment

Typeset in 11/17pt Book Antiqua
by Wiltshire Associates Publisher Services Ltd. Printed and bound in Great Britain
by Printondemand-Worldwide, Peterborough PE2 6XD

By the same author

The Great Gale of 1871
The Burton Agnes Disaster

Contents

To my mother, Sandra. You believed in me.

Foreword

The Lockington train crash occurred on Saturday, 26th July, 1986, when a train from Bridlington was in collision with a vehicle at the unmanned crossing at Lockington, East Yorkshire, resulting in the deaths of nine people. This is the first fatal crossing crash to take place on the Bridlington to Hull line since the Burton Agnes crash in 1947.

This book is an overdue memorial to those who died and for those who survived, and also for those who still live with the memories and consequences of that day. Lockington remains one of the forgotten disasters and its victims have had to live and suffer alone all these years.

Our thanks and congratulations have to go to Richard M Jones for writing this book and recording our memories of that day and for his valiant efforts in securing the funds for a permanent memorial to those who died.

Richard Myerscough
Survivor
Lockington Train Crash Support Group
August 2010

Author's Note

On 12th August 2009, I stood in front of an audience of people, not a huge crowd, but an interested few. I was launching my first book, *The Great Gale*, a tale told only in the small seaside resort of Bridlington, my home town. The story had captivated me from the moment I heard it when I was still at school, and as I grew older I knew that stories like these should not be forgotten. For six years I ploughed through archives, libraries and old newspaper reports looking for incredible stories of long lost heroes and wrecked ships. It was in February 1871 that hundreds of ships were caught in a storm off Bridlington, sinking 28 of them, killing 50 people and rendering the two lifeboats useless. After pursuing several leads to different mysteries I was the first person to find a Great Gale artefact from the site of one of the beached wrecks in over 130 years. I placed a headstone on the grave of a lifeboatman who had survived the day's events only to be forgotten about over time, and I was the first person to actually bring the story to print. The feedback I had after the first few weeks was better than I had ever expected and made the whole thing well worth the effort.

So standing in front of people telling my story of the gale was the end of the project for me. Then I began telling them of my next projects – this time I wouldn't concentrate on just one, I would do four or five at once. This is because there are plenty of times when information dries up and the trail goes cold, or you may be playing the waiting game for the letters to arrive or the person of interest to phone you back.

I had a small list of specialities and halfway down was the Lockington train crash. Over the years I have been interested in disasters, lost relics, history and basically anything that has or had needed an investigation. So tucked away in my files were a few news cuttings on this train crash just 20 miles from where I lived. I had already visited the crash site years before, and like I do at every disaster site, I took a few photographs and looked for the memorial. At this point I realised that there was no memorial to this crash. In fact there was nothing there to say such a traumatic event had even took place. So I thought no more about it until late 2009 when I made this my priority project. I typed up a couple of leaflets and posted them around the village asking for any information, driving to the town of Driffield afterwards to see if they would be so kind as to put an article in the paper for me. What I didn't expect was the number of people willing to help me. Before too long I had phone calls and emails from all kinds of people. "I saw the crash," "I survived the crash," "I was a rescue worker"; the list was endless. Needless to say there were a few people who were not willing to talk about it and found it too traumatic even 23 years on to relive the events. This I understood fully and didn't pursue them any further. But when my idea for a permanent memorial was put forward, suddenly it was front page of the *Hull Daily Mail* and I was being interviewed for the local TV news programme *Look North*. So my quest to build a memorial and tell a story of the Lockington train crash was on. This is my finished work.

Chapter 1

A Calm Sunny Day

In the mid to late 1980's there was a spate of major disasters that shook Britain. From 1987 to 1989 the front pages of the newspapers were filled with the most horrifying images and devastating death tolls which would leave a bitter legacy in a lot of cases. First there was the capsizing of the ferry *Herald of Free Enterprise* off Zeebrugge in 1987 killing 193, followed by the Kings Cross tube station fire the same year killing 31. 1988 saw the demise of the oil rig *Piper Alpha* (167 dead), the Clapham train crash (35 dead) and the bombing of Pan Am flight 103 over the small Scottish town of Lockerbie over the Christmas holidays (all 259 on the plane and 11 on the ground killed). Just weeks later, 1989 saw a second airliner crash on the M1 motorway at Kegworth (47 killed) and in the summer the ramming and sinking of the pleasure boat *Marchioness* on the River Thames (52 killed). It seemed every few months there was a new disaster, a new reason not to use that type of transport, a new company that was being negligible in their duty to the public safety.

Over 20 years have now passed since these disasters, but many people forget the lesser tragedies, the disasters that happen with a death toll in single figures. It is unfortunate that because there are more survivors, there are more people who are traumatised for the rest of their lives, more people who end up having psychological problems and in the meantime they too are forgotten. One of these disasters is the Lockington train crash. To many who remember the big ones, Lockington may seem insignificant and not worthy of having any attention, especially now. Who would even remember it?

Lockington happened long before any of those mentioned above. It was summer 1986, a time when the railways were run by British Rail, the Prime Minister was Margaret Thatcher, and an unlikely band of heroes would meet for the first time in a small East Yorkshire village.

* * * *

It was Saturday 26th July 1986, a calm, bright and sunny day in East Yorkshire. The schools had closed for the summer and many people were making the most of the time off and the good weather while it lasted. British summers are notorious for being short and to have warm sunshine on a day off was something not to be taken for granted.

The town of Bridlington sits on the East Yorkshire coast, surrounded by green fields and small villages. With the history of the town running into hundreds of years, it had also built a reputation up as a holiday destination for people further inland, particularly those from West and South Yorkshire. At this time of year the roads coming into Bridlington are normally full at the best of times, but on arriving into the town centre, the traffic comes to a standstill for a level crossing and it was here that trains running between Hull and Scarborough would cross. The track would give enough space for both inbound and outbound trains to pass at the same time, sometimes meeting side by side in Bridlington where they would pick up more passengers. The fact that two trains would use the level crossing within minutes would be a factor in the lot of irate drivers even today.

The station at Bridlington is situated on the outskirts of the town centre next to a major supermarket, and holding its own car park and taxi rank. Inside is a hall that would include a ticket office and benches for passengers to wait if it was too cold to wait outside. Through another set of doors would be three platforms. Over the bridge would be where you would wait if you wanted the Scarborough train, whereas if you wanted to go in the direction of Hull, Driffield or Beverley you would have a choice of two platforms. On the right would be the train from Scarborough, on the left would be the train which ran direct to and from Hull and terminated at the buffers. It was here at these buffers on that Saturday that the 0933 train to Hull was waiting. Four carriages made up the train, the front and back were Class 105's, the middle two were Class 114's or the driving cars. They were DMU's, or diesel multicoupler units, around 20-30 years old, very tough, very well built. Also, from what travellers said about them, very noisy also.

* * * *

Hilary Harbron was going to go by train this morning to collect her car from the Fiat garage in Hull. Her normal job was working for East Yorkshire Borough Council, and today was a day off. With the weather being a nice sunny and warm day, she decided she would walk from her house in Martongate to the train station, a journey of around a mile. The plan was to travel to Cottingham where her friends would meet her and take her to her car; afterwards they would invite her back to their home and have some lunch.

Arriving at the station, she boarded the train in the second carriage. A thought crossed her mind that the carriage was very old and pondered going to sit in the fourth carriage instead, but as it was about to leave she thought she would stay where she was. She sat on the right hand side of the carriage facing the direction of travel. She was not a frequent traveller by train, in fact it was very rare she even took the train.

* * * *

The Thorpe family – Kathleen and Brian, and their four children Gordon, Laura, Susan and Leona – had just spent a relaxing week in Bridlington on holiday. Today they were going back to Leicester by train and had actually planned to get the next train out, but they were early and the 0933 was already sat there waiting. So they got on and sat down in carriage four right at the back. Because of the number of people in the carriage they couldn't sit together and so Kathleen and Susan sat together on an opposite seat. It would be several hours until they got to Leicester with more changes to go through, so the family packed their luggage in the racks above and got a pack of cards out.

* * * *

A family from Barnsley who had also had a week's holiday in Bridlington were the O'Brien's. Elva, 52, was with her daughters Helen O'Brian, 24, and Maureen Sugden, 27, with her three grandchildren Adrien Sugden, aged eight, Jamie O'Brien, 18 months, and Lee Nicholson aged nine. Lee's mother Margaret was not with them on this journey. Elva, Helen and Jamie all lived together and after a nice relaxing week in a caravan near the cliff tops, they were heading home via Doncaster. They were due to get a train at half past ten but they had set off earlier than expected and saw the 0933 waiting there. They boarded in carriage four and took their seats in three lots of two seats with their backs facing direction of travel. They carried a fair bit of luggage, including a push chair, but soon stored them away and settled down waiting for departure. They noticed a few people running to get on board as it was now only minutes from departing.

Also in Bridlington that morning was a group of people setting off for Hull. School teacher Richard Myerscough, his wife Marion, their two children, 14-year-old Stephen and six-year-old David, were with another family friend Bill Shaw and his two children. Their aim was to take part in an anti-nuclear demonstration on behalf of the Green party against the nuclear waste dump at South Killingholme, Lincolnshire. They carried a huge banner which was rolled up and wrapped in its two poles.

As Richard walked onto the platform he hesitated, something stopping him in his tracks, a strange feeling. Normally they would sit in the front carriage with the children sitting on the front seats so they could look out of the windows leading to the driver's compartment and be able to see the track. For some reason today he decided against it and instead they were going to sit at the same spot but in the back carriage. The children could still see the track but it would be going behind them instead.

Notorious for being late, the Shaw's then arrived to join the party with just minutes to spare.

* * * *

Joining the train at Bridlington at the same time was Mary Foster, who was hoping for a relaxing day out on her own shopping in Hull. Normally she travelled by car but today she turned to her husband Fred and said: "I think I'll go on the train for a change." And on that note, Fred drove her down from their home in High Street to the station in his car. Arriving at the station, she bid goodbye to him and headed towards the waiting train, which was now almost ready to depart. Boarding the front carriage, she saw the train driver walking along the platform. She settled into her seat and watched a family with some children, who all seemed very excited at the day out.

This family is most likely to be Elsie and Herbert Marsters, their daughter and son-in-law Christine and Peter Quinn and their children Claire and Simon. They were returning to Hull after spending a week on holiday in Bridlington. Having quite a large and very close family, they would always stay at a house owned by relatives for the week and they did this every summer and had done for many years before. Herbert was a big fan of Hull rugby league club and followed them around, going to many of their matches. He had something else at the back of his mind over the next few days, as it was coming up to the first anniversary of his brother's death, although he would not let anything spoil the rest of the holiday for the family. They would return back to Hull in the next hour where Elsie and Herbert's nephew would collect them at the train station when they arrived.

* * * *

Sitting near Hilary Harbron in carriage two were two elderly sisters, Joan and Lorna Wilson. 73-year-old Joan from Bridlington and 68-year-old Lorna from Halifax had decided to go over to Beverley for the day as Lorna had come over to stay for a week's holiday. It was pure coincidence that Joan had married a man with the same surname as herself, Newton Wilson, who had built her a nice house with his own hands on Scarborough Road and she had lived in it ever since. She had moved over to Bridlington a long time ago but never lost touch with her family. Her three sons had also settled over here, her youngest Richard being a mechanic, Trevor joining the navy in the 1950's and later having a job building coaches at Scarborough, and her third son David was a journalist working in Surrey. (Normally Trevor would go up and see his mother on a Tuesday but this week he decided to leave her with his auntie and not interrupt.)

For 20 years Joan and Newton had run a guest house on Trinity Grove and she enjoyed every minute of it too. However things took a different turn when Newton died in 1979. She retired from running the guest house and she decided it was time to relax and enjoy herself. Today was a great day to go out with Lorna and they both chatted about different things as the train waited to depart from Bridlington station.

* * * *

58-year-old Peter Sturdy was the train guard for this journey. He had been in the job for 12 years and was officially working for British Rail out of the Botanic Gardens Motive Power Depot in Hull. A freight guard normally, today he was on overtime and that meant being passenger train guard, which he was more than happy with. His job was to make sure that all the doors were closed and to signal to driver Harry Brown, by using a push button, to start the train whenever they had stopped at a station. On top of that he did help passengers whenever they required assistance and generally made sure the journey went smoothly. He walked over to see Brown and confirmed with him the formation of the train and the stops they were to make. He walked back to his position and, after closing the outer doors, Sturdy went to his guard's compartment which was located in the third carriage. Now he could relax: he wasn't going to check or sell tickets to the passengers as they had all been bought at the ticket offices. It was an easy enough job and he enjoyed it. That morning he had worked a previous Bridlington-Hull trip, and arriving at Hull on the first leg Brown had asked for attention to be paid to the brakes of the first and third carriages. This was quickly sorted out and they were both happy to proceed. With around 100 people on board spread between the four carriages, the train was ready to go.

* * * *

Just as the whistle was about to blow, 15-year-old Amanda West ran onto the train in carriage four. Catching the train by literally a split second, she was going to see her friends in Beverley that she had grown up with in foster care. She took the last seat in the train facing backwards. As the train departed she could watch the track disappearing behind them. She had been singing a Wham song in her head all morning and as the train pulled away she continued going over the same tune, *Take me to the edge of Heaven.*

* * * *

At 0933 the train began its slow crawl out of Bridlington station. The next station stop was Nafferton, just a few miles down the line. Passing the abandoned stations of Burton Agnes and Lowthorpe, they would be stopping at Driffield, Hutton Cranswick, Beverley, Cottingham and finally Hull, less than an hour later. While Sturdy was in his cab, Harry Brown was driving the train. At 60 years old, he had 38 years experience on the railways and in that time had made a lot of friends. No-one ever seemed to have a bad word to say about Harry, and today he was in a better mood than ever. Wearing his blue British Rail uniform and with his brown bag next to him, he settled in for the routine journey. He had his lunch with him and a *Daily Mirror*. He always enjoyed doing the crossword in between journeys and today was no different. Now, as the train passed his house on Bessingby Road, he saw his wife holding his new born grandchild up at the window for him.

It took only a few minutes to reach Nafferton where the odd passenger would get on. Normally this would be a pretty quiet station although the village itself is deceptively large. With a quick check down the platform, the doors were closed and the train was on its way again. Although having only been on the journey for less than ten minutes, the passengers were settled into the usual routine of train-board life, chatting away to each other, making plans of what was to happen that day or that week. The bright sunny day offered a lot to a teenager on school holidays.

* * * *

Waiting on the platform in the small market town of Driffield was another bunch of travellers, waiting for the same train. 19-year-old Ian Simpson had been waiting for a friend to turn up so they could catch the early train to Beverley, but for some reason he had not turned up. Ian had now missed his train and, frustrated, he had waited for the next one so he could make the intended journey in order to be at his father's pub, the Oddfellows Arms, to start work. He had only just returned from a week's holiday in Marbella and wanted to give his father and step-mother some duty free that he had brought back. As the time was approaching ten to ten, he decided he would wait no further and, frustrated, he boarded the train. He put the bags on the seat next to him and relaxed, having his back in the direction of travel.

* * * *

Not too far away from Ian, two best friends were also waiting for the same train. 16-year-old Wayne Telling and 14-year-old Darren White were making the most of the school holidays. They had been friends for some years now, ever since Wayne's family had bought their house off Darren's family. Because Darren had only moved a few houses down, they got chatting and became good friends. That was seven years ago and both families were now pretty close to one another.

Wayne lived with his mother and stepfather, David and Jenny Carter, and was due to move house yet again on the Monday, so they had decided to go shopping in Hull together for some clothes as it may be the last time they would see each other as neighbours again, although they would still be close friends long after they had left Driffield. It was only the day before they had arranged to go out so it may have not come as a shock to see Wayne up and about just after 9am ready to go with his red and blue jumper on and a grey bomber jacket. Jenny called round to see Darren's mother Pam on the way into town and passed on that he was hoping to get the 9.50 train to Hull. However, Darren had other ideas and wanted to stay in bed a bit longer. Pam then went upstairs to drag him out of bed. "Wayne is ready and waiting so get yourself off."

On that note, he got up, put on his bluey-grey chords and yellow Pringle jumper, grabbed a bit of breakfast and made his way up the street to Wayne. Saying goodbye to his mother, Darren was met with the usual "Be careful . . . make sure you have plenty of money." Meeting Wayne, they headed down to the station together and planned the day ahead between them.

Wayne himself had had a bit of a hectic time recently since his family had decided to move. His step father David had got a new job and was looking forward to a fresh start. While the changes were happening, Wayne would stay in Northallerton with a friend. The plan was to get him into Northallerton Grammar school so he could get a full year to sort out his exams. While he was there, David would be in Middlesbrough staying with family, although he would pick Wayne up at the end of the week to spend time as a family again before work and school would force them to go their separate ways once again. Although things were up in the air, he did take his exams at Northallerton Grammar School, while David worked in Pickering. All this travelling around was unsettling at the best of times so having a steady job, school and home was, hopefully, not far from being a reality. Wayne would then spend time in Middlesbrough, supporting the football team there and even attending the matches as he was becoming quite a fan.

So now they had just days to go before the whole family moved to Norton, near Malton. They had chosen a house, Wayne had chosen his bedroom, and the removal people were booked and ready. He would miss living in Driffield without a doubt. He had got a good part-time job close by on a farm and, having left school, he had been accepted into Askham Bryan College of Agriculture to study and was taking his farming seriously. It wouldn't be long now until he would learn the results of his exams. Thanks to his job, thought, he now had some money to spend, and today he would spend that in Hull. His early morning starts to work on the wild oats were paying off at last.

They boarded the train and took their seats in the front carriage. Normally Wayne would sit by the window, but today Darren would sit at the window and Wayne would be in the aisle seat. The two lads chatted as normal and paid no real attention to anyone else around them.

* * * *

Not far behind Wayne and Darren were two other teenagers, 17-year-old Jason Schofield and his 16-year-old best friend Greg Addison. They were massive fans of snooker and had met a few years before at the Driffield Cricket Club and regularly played together. They were both pretty good at it and after a while they ended up hanging around together more and more. Having had won plenty of games and even represented Beverley in the Yorkshire league at one point, the two lads were obsessed with it, talking about it non-stop.

Jason and Greg had, on the Friday, decided to have a day out in Hull as Jason wanted to take some tennis shorts back to the shop as they didn't fit him, and Greg was looking to buy a motorcycle helmet. So that Saturday morning they had got up, dressed, grabbed their cash and headed to the station. Jason left his house on York Road wearing Lois chords, a Sergio Tachina t-shirt and a pair of Diadora trainers, carrying a bag with his shorts in and headed to meet Greg. Greg lived on Mill Falls nearby but it was easier to meet outside Martin's newsagent on the corner of Westgate, which was only down the road. He spotted his long-sleeve yellow shirt straight away and they headed down the main street to the station.

They realised that they were cutting it fine to catch the train so they ran down towards the platform, quickly getting their ticket from the office and ran over the bridge to the train, which was seconds from departing. They only just got on, boarding the front carriage, Jason sat at the front, just one group of seats behind the driver, in the aisle seat facing the direction of travel. Greg sat opposite on the window side. The rush was over, they too could relax now and let the train take them away, it should be a good day.

* * * *

A very popular Driffield girl, 23-year-old Annette Stork was boarding the train to go to Hull with her fiancé Herbert Donnelly and their one-year-old son Jordan. They were going to buy Jordan some new clothes with some birthday money – he had turned one year old on Monday 21st. Her niece, Michelle, should have gone with them that day but she had stayed at home with chickenpox.

When she had left school, Annette had always wanted to be a hairdresser and not long ago had managed to secure a position as an apprentice at Wray's Hairdressers. Although she had given up work after Jordan had been born she was due to return soon as it had been a while and she wanted to kick start her career again. She used to do her friends' hair to get the practice in and wasn't bad at it either! Having a lot of friends, she was well liked and had worked at Cindico's Nursery Products with some of her family, so she always had a good laugh at work. On top of that she had been going to college in Bridlington once a week doing hairdressing.

The family boarded the train and took their seats in carriage one.

* * * *

Also running to catch the train from Driffield was 21-year-old Sue Dales. It was a day off from her work at the Driffield branch of Lloyds Bank and she was heading to Hull for some last minute shopping for her holiday to Tenerife. It was her first-ever holiday abroad so she was looking forward to it. She wanted some new clothes and a few other things, so she should find what she is looking for in the city. There is only so much to buy in Driffield with it being a small town. Living at home with her parents in The Mount, like Jason and Greg, she had to run to catch the train and boarded it in the front carriage just as the doors were closing. Catching her breath she took a seat opposite Ian Simpson and settled down.

* * * *

The village of Hutton Cranswick is just outside Driffield, a very quiet place but, like the other small places up the line, it does have its own railway station. Normally on a train journey, very few people get on or off at this stop in comparison, but all the same the train would stop here for the odd passenger or two who lived there. Working that day at the signal box was 29-year-old Charles "Chaz" Walker. Having held this position for three years now, he had started work at 6am, arriving after the short journey from his home in Driffield. His first job of the day was to inform the signal boxes either side of him, which were Driffield and Beverley, that he was there and that the Hutton Cranswick signal box was now manned. Each signal box could have one section (the line in between signal boxes is known as a "section") and you are only allowed one train on a section at any one time, and the signalman's job is to make sure that that happens. Chaz's section until recently was from Hutton Cranswick to the next signal box at Lockington, then the next was from Lockington to Beverley North. When they had recently closed Lockington and Beverley North, his section changed to Hutton Cranswick all the way up to Beverley. It was a pretty quiet job, but certain aspects were enjoyable. Because he was on a station he sold tickets to passengers and handled queries, planned journeys and spoke to the train drivers, which made it a bit more interesting.

Today wasn't that busy, it was usually busier on a weekday with people going to and from work, but for a Saturday it was still early anyway. A lot of people would only be just getting out of bed after a week of early starts.

At around 0955 the train from Bridlington via Driffield rolled to a stop. The doors opened and Chaz went to say hello to the driver, Harry Brown. He had known Harry many years and always exchanged pleasantries. Today he was in a good mood after seeing his grandchild at the window back in Bridlington, and didn't waste a moment to tell Chaz all about it! However, the conversation was short lived as the trains only spend a minute or so in the station before heading on their way. At this point there are no other trains on the line so they are always cleared to go whenever they are ready and the doors are closed. Waving goodbye to Harry, Chaz then went back to his signal box to tap out two bells to Beverley. This told the Beverley box that the train had just left his station and was on its way to their end. At the same time, the train from Hull had departed Beverley so he got two bells back. The two trains would cross each other just a few minutes down the line and most likely wave at each other when passing.

* * * *

So speeding down the line at around 60 miles per hour, the four carriages of the 0933 Bridlington to Hull train was over half-way through its journey. Families going for a day out, young and old alike, talking, laughing, discussing their week with each other.

Jason Schofield and Greg Addison had by now settled

into their journey, and decided to count their money at this point, to see how much they had on them. No doubt their thoughts were filled with the up and coming shopping trip and, nine times out of ten, snooker.

There was a normal cheery air on the train with normal chatter and friendly banter. The thoughts of spending money in a shopping trip. The beautiful hot summer's day. A perfect day to spend outdoors. With 64 passengers and two crew on board, the train was less than ten minutes to Beverley. And just three minutes to a level crossing at the tiny village of Lockington.

Wayne Telling wearing the jumper he wore the day he died.

Wayne at Darren White's house, 1986.

Wayne and Darren together in 1983.

Darren White. A school photo taken in 1986.

Joan Wilson (far left) and her sister Lorna (second from right) at a wedding.

Far Left:
Joan Wilson on holiday.

Sue Dales

Annette Stork holding
baby Jordan.

Richard Myerscough and family.

Wayne Harman, aged eight.

The Thorpe family.

Train guard Peter Sturdy a year before
the crash enjoying a holiday away.

Sue Dale's
train ticket

Darren White's
train ticket
(child's price).

A Class 105 carriage. The train at Lockington had two
of these - carriages one and four.

Harry Brown driving a train past Beverley Park.

A train waits to depart from Bridlington station in the mid-1980s. It is a scene such as this that greeted travellers on the morning of 26 July 1986.

Departing Bridlington, driver Harry Brown waved to his newly born grandchild in the window of his home which was just behind the bridge in front.

Chaz Walker in Hutton Cranswick signal box. He was working here on the day of the disaster.

The entrance to the quiet village of Lockington today.

Lockington Station, March 1982. Just months before the crash the signal box and barrier had been removed.

Lockington level crossing today approaching from Beverley. The photographs are taken about where the train came to rest following the collision with the van, which had emerged onto the road from in between the two houses.

Chapter 2

"There's been a train smash"

Just eight miles from Driffield on the A164 road to
Beverley, there is a cross-roads that if you weren't looking
for it you would probably miss. Approaching from
Driffield, if you turned right you would be on the
country road that led to the tiny village of Lockington, a
population of just over 500. If you turned left you would
be heading towards the even smaller village of Aike
(pronounced "ache").

It is this road that leads also to the Lockington level
crossing, one of 10,000 of such crossings in Britain.
Passing a few farm houses, the crossing is nothing special
and you would not think twice about it once you had
passed over it. Over the crossing, the road narrows and
winds towards Aike, passing a turn off to the (even
smaller still) village of Wilfholme. This is the level
crossing that the train approached, having two lines, one

for the train heading away from Beverley and the other for the one heading to Beverley.

Trains had passed this very spot for decades; there was even a station here at one point, which had closed in June 1960. The old station house, situated right next to the crossing, is still there but for many years it has been a privately owed residence.

Until December 1985 the crossing had been manned, but due to cut back in British Rail funding, it was now classed as an automatic crossing, where the approaching train would trigger sensors to make the alarm sound and the warning lights flash. Unlike the more busier main road crossings, this one had no barriers. It was known as an AOCR, or Automatic Open Crossing Remotely-Monitored, and it gave the driver no less than 37 seconds warning that a train was approaching. At 1280 yards away the amber warning light will show for three seconds, followed by 34 seconds of flashing twin red lights.

These particular types of crossing had only been introduced in 1983, and there had been a lot of concern from the locals of these surrounding villages over the lack of barriers. More than once there had been near disasters and even trains derailing. It would not take much for an animal to stray onto the line or a car blocking the track to disrupt the whole line or cause a major incident. On top of that, nobody trusted the warning lights. People had previously complained that the alarms had sounded yet no train had come. Some even claimed that the train had passed and the lights failed to work. Whatever the faults, it was cost-cutting by British Rail that was causing these changes, and this was just one crossing on one line. How many more lines were there to be concerned about? But these particular lights had been checked just three days previously and everything was seen to be working correctly. This didn't stop the whole situation being a disaster waiting to happen. The work to complete the automation of the East Coast line was only half way through and BR still had eleven more crossings to work on.

Just behind the old station house were two others, called the Railway Cottages. Living in No. 1 was 42-year-old cattle dealer Malcolm Ashley, his wife Margaret and their foster son, 11-year-old Wayne Harman.

Wayne had been taken into care by them in April after a breakdown of his family due to various rows involving his mother Ethel's heavy drinking. Ethel had married Heinz Meinke in 1979 and when just a year later he died, Wayne adopted his surname Meinke (pronounced Men-ka), although legally his name was still Harman. For Wayne's natural father Barrie Harman, it was a painful decision to allow his sons to be placed in care but there was nothing he could do now. If Wayne wanted to seek him when he was old enough then he would be welcomed with open arms. Until that day, Barrie had to continue and live his life with his new wife and family. The Ashley's were only supposed to have Wayne for four days but that was extended indefinitely and he soon settled in as one of the family.

Ashley had been driving for 26 years and was well aware of the train lines in the surrounding villages. That morning Wayne got into the blue Ford Escort van which was sitting outside the front door for the intended journey towards Aike to see a member of Malcolm's family, like they did every week. Once all today's jobs were done, Wayne was going to Beverley to play in a football match. So, with their black Labrador Chad in the back, Malcolm started the van, backed up, gave his neighbour a friendly wave and drove out towards the main road. It was 10am.

* * * *

On the train, passenger Sue Dales in carriage one stood up for some reason. She might have wanted to dust herself down or just straighten her clothes, she doesn't know. But as she did, she looked out of the dri-ver's cab window and for a split second caught sight of Ashley's blue van crossing the path of the train. There was nothing anybody could do, the train slammed into the van at around 60 mph. Those who could, braced themselves and held on. The rest of the people who didn't see the danger would not be so fortunate.

* * * *

Eight-year-old Lee Nicholson stood up in carriage four. "Gran," he said to Elva O'Brien, "I want to go to the toilet." She told him to go down the carriage and it wouldn't be far way. Moments later he was back. "Gran, I can't find the toilet."

She then turned to him and said: "Well sit down and I will come with you and find one in a minute." This was a small insignificant decision that would save their lives.

* * * *

Richard Myerscough was reading a book. All of a sudden, and for some unknown reason, he decided to stop reading and instantly put the book down. He had another funny feeling, one that made him on edge slightly, as if he was expecting something bad to happen. He didn't believe in premonitions, but something just didn't let go and he mentally prepared for whatever was to come. At that moment, the people on the train heard an almighty bang and felt the whole train shudder. Looking out of the fourth carriage, Richard could see the train snaking along the track from side to side. Amanda West clung on to the seat for dear life; she knew the trains were noisy and swayed anyway but this was something else. She heard chaos and screaming behind her, watching the track from all angles. She was terrified. Something had happened, something bad. But worse was to come.

Elva O'Brien shouted to Maureen and Helen to grab the kids and hold on to them tight. As sparks and debris flew up and hit the windows, the expressions on their faces told a thousand words. Something was going very wrong. Lee ended up on the floor but holding on to the steel bars under the seats as the carriage was rolling, getting worse.

* * * *

In carriage three, train guard Peter Sturdy saw the needle of the vacuum pressure gauge for the brakes suddenly fall. It was only moments ago he had noticed that it was at its correct reading of 21in. and now in an instant he knew something was wrong. Either there was something seriously wrong or the driver had applied the brakes in an emergency. Then he felt a shudder and a vibration coming from up forward. The carriage was being thrown from side to side and came off the rails. He braced himself for a collision. At this point, only a couple of people realised that the train had been in a collision with Ashley's van. As far as people were concerned this was a derailment and there could possibly be another train involved.

* * * *

In carriage two, Hilary Harbron realised something was definitely wrong when the whole train began to shudder. As the movement became more violent, she was thrown out of her seat and onto the floor. But this was nothing compared to what was happening at the front. The second carriage was now ripped away from the first and continuing down the line at a crazy angle. If the people in cars two, three and four were scared, then the occupants of the first carriage were in hell itself.

* * * *

In the first carriage all hell had broken loose. As driver Harry Brown was raising his arm to protect his face, Ian Simpson was suddenly wedged in his seat, a fluke that amazingly saved his skin. For a split second it was all too unreal to take in and he wondered what was happening. Looking out of the window he found it bizarre how he could actually see the train tracks running down the line. *The front carriage is actually going sideways down the line!* he thought. At that very second the whole carriage upturned and smashed over on its side, all the windows exploding with fragments of glass and gravel. His legs fell into the gap where the window was. Amazingly still being forced back into his seat, he was bouncing his feet on the dirt track that was now underneath the upturned train. Sue Dales sitting opposite him fell into the window space and was thrown around like a rag doll, tumbling over and spinning around as if she was nothing more than clothes in a washing machine.

Darren White and Wayne Telling didn't even have time

to hold onto their seat. They both shouted: "Oh f…k!" as they started getting thrown around in their seat. The first thing they knew that something was wrong was when a huge amount of gravel being thrown up at the windows. As the train jerked, Darren's head slammed against the glass and he lost consciousness.

Jason Schofield shouted over to Greg: "Hold on mate!" and grabbed on to the hand rest as tight as he could. Shards of glass and stones were showering his face at a massive rate and cutting him all over. Greg was launched out of his seat and fell into the window void and was instantly crushed. Jason followed him but incredibly he missed the hole by inches. He struck his head and was immediately knocked unconscious. At this point Sue was still being thrown around but she didn't go under the carriage. She was by now unconscious and terribly injured, but alive. Ironically she can be classed as being one of the lucky ones. The fact she was in that state and completely unconscious saved her from a scene that has since left many survivors with mental scars over two decades on. The train was still moving on its side with gravel showering the passengers, Ian thinking *when is this thing going to end?* Finally, after what seemed a long time but was probably only about 20 seconds, the front carriage came to a halt. The carriage was full of dirt, rocks, blood, limbs and people, dazed and confused. It was now a fight for survival, to get out of the train before anything else happened. Would another train hit them? Would the fuel tanks explode and engulf them all? It would seem extremely bitter that they had survived all this just to have another life-threatening menace prey on them. Everyone had the same kind of idea, whether injured or not – get out of the train.

* * * *

The Thorpe family held on while the train snaked across the track. They saw the gravel shooting up at the window and several things hitting the side of the train. This was confusing as they had no idea they had suffered a collision. Suddenly the luggage above came down and struck Gordon on the side of his face, nine-year-old Susan had her playing cards scattered all over the floor and as the train came to a stop they began picking them up.

* * * *

In the end carriage, Richard Myerscough was holding on to his family for all he could. There erupted suddenly a big cloud of dust, a bit like a fog, caused by the crashing train going all over the track and embankments. He leaped across and jumped on his two boys, grabbing them and pushing them into the seat. Bill Shaw couldn't get a lift out of his seat, he was frozen solid to it. Marian had been at the time talking to Bill when they were stopped in conversation. Now there was complete bewilderment, no-one understanding what was going on. All they knew at this moment is that whatever had caused this, it started with one hell of a crunch. Their train came to a rest, the carriage obviously by now was no longer on the rails but at an angle, tilting sideways slightly. Then there was just a deathly silence. Nobody was screaming or crying. It took a few seconds for people to gather their thoughts and realise that this was reality and that they were now in a very bad situation. All of a sudden, bursting through the door, was the guard Peter Sturdy, running into carriage four and running back out the same door just as quickly.

* * * *

Next door to the old station house lived farmers Bob and Mary Bayes. They had not long just finished feeding the cattle and were sitting down with a relaxing cup of tea. It was hard work looking after the farm, as any Yorkshire farmer would tell you, and when it was tea time, it was tea time and nothing would disturb them. That was until they suddenly heard a loud, deep rumbling. At first they just though it was heavy farm traffic on the level crossing, and thought no more about it. Cattle wagons often go over the railway lines and it sounded like that was exactly what the noise was. It was only about a minute later their next door neighbour Maureen Lunn ran in through the open back door.

"You'd better come outside," said the shocked Mrs Lunn.

"Why? What's the matter?"

"There's been a train smash!"

"Don't talk silly, Maureen," was Bob's reply.

"Genuine, come on out."

Not really believing what she had just said, they ran out of the door and looked across at the railway line over the field. They couldn't believe what they were seeing.

* * * *

Working as a postman, and nearly at the end of his delivery, Brian Mellony had been out in his van on his usual round by about 7am that morning. He had worked his way from Skerne Road, Driffield, down the farms and villages and working backwards and forwards several times over the train line at Lockington. He had already passed over the line about six times in just a few hours, but that was normal for him, sometimes you had to back track with the roads branching off and winding in different directions. Normally he would finish the round at Scorborough, which was just up the road, and it would be back home to Driffield.

By 10am he had just passed over the Lockington crossing after delivering to Station House and Railway Cottages and was now on the way to Aike, heading down the road and delivering to the first farm on the left, about 200 yards away. Making his way back down the farm's path to the main road, he had the window down and suddenly heard a big bang. Not knowing what it was, he looked across in the direction of the noise and saw a big dusty cloud of gravel. To his horror, he could see it was a train rearing up. Shocked by what he saw, he drove down to the road and instead of turning left to Aike, he headed straight back to the railway track. As he approached the crossing, he saw that the warning lights were flashing and the alarm was still activating. His first concern was getting the emergency services told as quick as possible, so he crossed the track, knocked on Maureen Lunn's door to get her to ring the emergency services, which she did immediately.

* * * *

It now became obvious that there had been a major train derailment. Although it took just seconds, the collision happened like this......

When Malcolm Ashley drove out of his yard in his blue Ford Escort van to visit his family, he turned left to head towards Aike. The crossing lights and alarms were seen by several witnesses that day to be working fine, but for some reason or other he was oblivious to them, whether he was distracted by the dog or whether the bright sunshine of that hot day made the lights unclear to see. Whatever the reason, the van went across the line at the exact moment the train was passing. The front of the first carriage struck the van and immediately derailed, ripping the vehicle up and sending it off in five different pieces up the left side of the track. A large scar appeared in the field to the left of the Hull-bound track where carriage one shot out and was then pulled back leaving various debris in the grass. As the train careered up the line sideways, dirt and pieces of track were kicked up into the air and all carriages were swaying around before carriage one flipped over onto its side and was dragged backwards along the side of the track bed. When the local eyewitnesses went to the crash site, the mayhem was apparent. Carriage number one was on its side, lying down the gravel embankment pointing in the direction of where it had just come from, Carriage number two was upright still but lying across both rail lines, the end of the carriage ending up in a bush pointing into the next field. The back two carriages were still attached to the number two carriage but were in a zig-zag shape next to the upturned number one carriage. The van was barely recognisable as a vehicle, so much so that most people didn't even realise that a vehicle had been involved. Wreckage and bodies were scattered along the line. When you come upon a disaster site such as this it beggars the burning question – Where do you start?

Chapter 3

The rescue

Acting Sergeant Keith Ralphs of Humberside Police had been in the force for seven years and enjoyed his job, spending most of his serving time in Hull City Centre. However, for three months now he had been at Beverley due to staff shortages. On this Saturday morning he had started work at 7am and would always have a briefing first thing, giving his colleagues a run-down of things that were happening in the area, such as stolen cars, people in the cells or any recent developments. The day before he had been looking at 22-year-old WPC Carol Ann Dyson's traffic accident report and figured she needed a bit of guidance on how to write these reports better. Carol was just finishing her two years' probationary period with Humberside Police and was in charge of the rural car, covering around Beverley, where she lived at the time, right up to Driffield. Keith said to his colleagues that if she is called to another traffic accident then to make sure he went with her so he can show her the correct way. Also in Beverley was a control room, manned by a Sergeant, a PC and a civilian to man the phones and direct the other officers to whichever incident deserves what attention. Just after 10am the first 999 calls came in from Lockington and Keith was immediately called in the admin offices round the back of the police station. One of them had turned to Carol and said: "Can you go to the level crossing at Lockington? A train has collided with a car." She turned to the map and looked to see where Lockington was, figured out that this could be pretty serious and raced to her car. She started the engine and immediately put her foot down and headed away to the crash site.

Keith saw the same crew and they basically said that there had been some kind of accident at Lockington and they had sent WPC Dyson, so on that note he got up and went to his car to follow her on his own. He walked out of his office and it was at this point that they radioed him for a second time, asking him if he was in his car yet and could he hear the force radio. He replied that no he was not in the car yet…. "You'd better hurry up, there's a train involved," came the reply, to which he ran to the car and sped off with blue flashing lights going but no sirens.

At the same time, over in Hull, PC Dale Turrell was driving a riot van over to Queens Gardens with several officers in the back, ready to give a hand to other officers dealing with things like shoplifting. He drove from Gordon Street station just after 10am and as they were driving off there was a call over the radio from the force ops room at Queens Gardens. "There has been a derailment at Lockington, there are no injuries, it is a goods train." This he thought was unusual as you do not regularly see goods trains on the line during the day. However they were sent to Beverley station at New Walk just to stand by in case they needed extra manpower. As they arrived in Beverley, the other officers all went into the building while Dale was asked to get a CID car ready. It was clear that the severity of the crash was not yet known. Four of the men were told to sit down and wait, on stand by in case they were needed, while Dale took the unmarked beige coloured Mark 3 Ford Escort car with a "major incident box" in the back just in case, and sped to the scene of the crash.

45-year-old Police Constable Bill Sullivan was on duty at Driffield station when the first call came through. He had been in the force for 17 years and had previously done a further 12 years with the RAF police. The biggest things he had had to contend with in his career had been the Toxteth riot in July 1981 and the miners dispute of 1984/85. But this one seemed a lot more serious, although at first it was automatically assumed that the crash was at Driffield crossing as there was no indication that it was anywhere else. A few minutes later he was told that it was somewhere in between Driffield and maybe Hutton Cranswick. "That's a hell of a lot of crossings!" came his reply.

It soon became apparent that it was at the Lockington crossing on the main line, although Bill didn't have a vehicle. A traffic police patrol car then picked him up and he was driven away by PC Holliday to the scene of the crash down the road towards Beverley. The scene was only six miles away and it looked like they would be first on scene.

Over near Brough, around 20 miles from the crash site, was Bishop Burton beat police officer PC Howard Brown. Having been in the service for nine years, he was down there on his own to do something trivial like re-issuing a firearms certificate, when it came over the radio of the crash. He knew straight away that the crossing involved was not in Lockington village but towards Aike, so he took off towards the scene. Being so far away, it would take him 25 minutes to get there, still being one of only a few officers that had managed to get there first.

* * * *

Bob Brown had been an ambulance man for ten years and today he would be enjoying his day off. And what a great day to have off too, a nice day with the bright, hot sun. By mid morning that day he was at home in

Driffield preparing to go out shopping with his wife Edith when the phone rang downstairs in the hallway. It was Colin, one of the lads who worked for him who said: "There's been a train crash at Lockington, get yourself there!" Without even thinking, his reply was a cool "I'm on my way."

Although it was not unusual to be called in from home, a train crash was a definite exception and certainly not a normal call. He went back upstairs to get changed and told Edith the news. "I've got to go, there's been a train crash."

It didn't take long to sort himself out, and Edith took him to Driffield Ambulance Station where his colleague Tony Capes was washing an ambulance from a previous job. The information was so fresh that Tony hadn't even heard about it yet with him only just arriving back himself. "Someone's pulling my leg!" said Bob. "Someone's just told me there's been a train crash at Lockington." The truth was confirmed immediately and out of the four first line vans that were sitting there, he took the first one he came to and sped off down Victoria Road. With sirens going full belt and clear roads ahead, Bob raced to the crossing. It was just ten minutes into the disaster.

* * * *

Barry Skelton had joined the fire service in 1962 and was sub-officer in charge, a position he'd held since April

1978. Known as B division station 4 (or B4) based in Driffield, they were only part-time firemen, Barry being a printer by trade. The most notable fire he had ever had to attend was the aftermath of the 1974 Flixborough explosion, a time when the fire was so long and ferocious that crews had to rotate from all over the Humber region. That task had taken over a month long, and had seen mass casualties resulting from the main explosion and subsequent fire, but other than that big one it was mostly farm fires and much smaller incidents they dealt with.

At the time of the crash he was up at Dee Atkinson's showfield near Driffield where they were having a timber sale. His bleeper went off and his first thought was *typical – it goes off when I'm right down here!* He raced back to the fire station at Driffield where he was told, like everyone else rushing to the scene, that there was a train crash at Lockington. At this time no other information was available. How serious it was would only be revealed when the first rescuers got there.

He could see already that one pump (or fire engine) had just pulled out and was heading to the scene. Barry was on the second pump that went, about ten minutes behind the first one. (With hindsight had they realised how big this was they would have sent everything in one go but information was only filtering in slowly.) Each engine carried six people, two in the front, four in the back.

Travelling to the scene with Barry Skelton was his colleague Malcolm Gill. It was not long after 10am when he too had got the call. Like Barry, his pager went off, and when it bleeps you just go straight to the fire station where a paper message would be seen giving whatever details of the incident that was available. Malcolm had been in the fire service for 11 years and had attended the derailment ten years previous at Kilnwick when 25-year-old farmer Charles Shaw was killed by a train striking his car. When he wasn't fighting fires he ran his own business doing repairs for garden machinery and horticultural equipment.

Sitting in the back listening to the radio reports coming over was fire-fighter Dave Smith, who had already seen eight years in the service while at the same time running his furniture design business from just around the corner.

The 999 calls had reached their destinations and within minutes there was a flurry of activity. Police, fire engines and ambulances were all on their way. For the people in the train, they had just minutes left to wait for rescue. But those minutes, for them, were dragging. The rescue couldn't come quick enough.

* * * *

Over at Hutton Cranswick station, Chaz Walker was in the middle of talking to the operator at Beverley via the internal phone. They were chatting about all sorts of things when they both realised that both trains were slightly late. This was unusual for this to happen and neither station be aware of any hold-up on the line. The Beverley train should have been here by now, Chaz said to him. At that moment the Beverley operator said: "Oh hang on, I've got a phone call coming through from one of the crossing phones."

He was gone only a moment when he came back on the line and said: "There's been a crash!" to which he immediately sent the "line blocked" signal to signify that the line had been shut down. They both hung up and Chaz went outside to put explosive detonators on the line to warn any train to stop as soon as possible and not go any further. This would have been highly unlikely but he laid them just in case. The idea of detonators was that they make a loud bang when the train runs over them and when the driver hears them it signals the train to stop for emergency or safety reasons. For Chaz, there was nothing he could do now but advise passengers on the situation unfolding. At this moment in time, still nobody knew how bad the crash was.

* * * *

In the wrecked train, Richard Myerscough, his family and friends got up to leave the carriage. They exited on the left side and went straight down the embankment and into some bramble bushes. His first thought was that they had hit another train as he saw a train facing the other way, not realising it was the first carriage, which originally he was intending to travel in. With them all congregating on the dirt road next to the track, Bill Shaw disappeared, running back up the track towards the level crossing so somebody would alert the emergency services. He managed to get to the crossing phone but when he told the operator that there had been a rail crash he couldn't tell them where they were. He then headed back towards the crash, checking two bodies on the line that are now known to be Malcolm Ashley and Wayne Harman. Incredibly, he saw that although they were motionless, both were still alive and breathing. He put Wayne into the recovery position so as not to choke and went back to the carriages.

At this time, Richard went back to the wreckage and entered the third carriage, taking his son Stephen with him. He knew that somewhere in there was rescue equipment he could use. He found where it was straight away, smashed open a box to get out the first aid kit, grabbed a fire extinguisher and some tools and went off to see if he could help anyone. It was about this time that the first people were emerging from the upturned first carriage. Getting on to that carriage was very difficult as it was on its side, minus the wheels. The doors always open outwards so people were now struggling to open them and push them upwards, which was twice as hard with the weight of the doors, being so high up, and the fact that there were a lot of injuries suffered by those who were trying.

A French girl suddenly appeared. She was a French exchange student, Anne Gagnier, who was staying with the Moon family in Driffield. Then the two teenage Moon sisters, Emma and Sarah, appeared and sat on top of the carriage with their legs dangling over the now vertical roof. One of them had a badly injured foot, both girls suffering from shock.

All this time, one of the engines that continually drive the train forward in carriages two and three was still running. Richard heard the engines, "revving away like mad," due to the gearbox being smashed up. At that moment he dived under the train and there it was – the engine revving its heart out. Next to the engine there was a box with buttons, so he thought *Well, if I press one of these buttons then the engines are bound to stop.* The first button he pressed had no result but he carried on and kept pressing buttons until the engines stopped dead. As far as he was concerned there shouldn't be the engine going as it's a danger even though it was diesel and it won't easily catch fire. With the engine going quiet, he focused on entering carriage two, but upon walking through the carriage, he realised there was nobody there who needed any help and left again.

It was now that he decided to enter the upturned carriage number one. The only way in was the door which had been attached to carriage number two. When he wrestled with the wrecked door and managed to squeeze in, the sight that greeted him was horrendous.

* * * *

Ian Simpson was bewildered. *What the f**k has just happened*, he thought. Once the train had stopped he put his feet into the window hole and stood up. He looked up at the seats in the opposite aisle, now taking on the role as the roof. He looked down at the unconscious girl; this was too real to be a dream, he thought. Shocked by the suddenness and violence of it all, he took a moment to get his head together and figure out what he should do, what his next move would be. He heard a voice calling for help, coming from underneath the train. He looked under the train out of the window void and saw Greg Addison dying, but could not be reached. Helpless to do anything, the only thing he could say was: "I'm sorry, I can't do anything." Even Ian and ten other strong men wouldn't be able to lift the 24-ton train and get him out. He went to see what other help he could offer.

* * * *

Jason Schofield woke up not long after in the void of the window with dirt and grass all around him. He turned and saw Greg trapped under the train groaning. He was still alive and literally right next to him, but again there was nothing he could do. He grabbed Greg's head and tried to move his face, he tried pulling his hand and shoulder but he wouldn't move. In what would haunt him for years to come, he says to this day that he saw that "The last bit of life drained out of him in front of my eyes."

In deep shock, he then moved around the carriage, seeing the body of Helen Lodge close by, and went to give the Moon sisters a hand getting up out of the carriage. They then sat on the top of the carriage together, unable yet to make it down onto the ground. Jason jumped off and helped a few people down by getting their feet in his hands. All he could do now was get out of the way. But as he started walking to the crossing, he started losing his eye-sight and the feeling in his hands. He would open his eyes and it would be black. This was later found out to be not an injury but down to shock, but that didn't stop him being terrified at going blind. Hundreds of emotions were going through him all at the same time. He had just witnessed a major crash, seen his friend die under the train and witnessed death and injury on a large scale, all in the space of a few minutes. It was a very surreal moment, so he turned around and looked back at the wreckage and lifeless bodies that littered the tracks. Only now was he realising how real everything was.

* * * *

Pushing a door above his head, Ian Simpson pulled himself out of the train and stood upright. He saw the rest of the train at different angles and at this point other people had already begun to start climbing out too. He slid off the roof and sat in the cornfield with the other survivors. He had no injuries, which was a miracle considering he was in the worst possible place. In fact he was in good shape, that he was sure of, so now he got up again and wanted to go back and help others. Were there any other dangers? Was the train in peril of catching fire?

He then heard people screaming for help. So climbing on top of the carriage again he jumped back in to see if there was anything he could do. He tried to go back to the young man trapped underneath (Greg Addison), even digging with his bare hands to try and free him. It was no use, he was now unconscious and it was obvious that he wouldn't make it. The injuries to the other passengers were horrific. Glass had been thrown around when the windows were blown out and there were all kinds of cuts, broken arms, even hair hanging off some passengers where they had been virtually scalped.

Another man, Mark Hullah, had his right arm trapped through a window going under the train. Again there was nothing at hand to be able to move him and for the time being he had to stay there. With the weight of the carriage, there would be no way this could be lifted without the use of a crane. However, Ian carried on walking around the carriage, and as he got to the door he noticed a young boy, Simon Quinn, with his legs trapped in the door with gravel and ballast from the track scooped up. Movement of the train made the ballast slide even more and he grabbed the door so no more would go on his legs. As more of this was falling down it was trapping the door onto the boy's legs and he was in immediate danger of having them severed off. This is where Ian met fellow passenger Len Robinson, who came to his assistance. They worked together to dig out his legs and pull the door up. So much effort was needed that Ian could feel the ball joint coming out of its socket in his arms. Luckily, at this point a fire-fighter was on scene and quickly wedged a hydraulic ram under the door. Ian let go and the lad was freed in just a few minutes. If it wasn't for the quick actions of these two men, Simon would have lost his legs. Now the emergency services had arrived, he could step aside and let them do their job. He walked back through the train and jumped back out again. A fireman did stop and thank him for his help as he made his way back down the track. It was now very quiet as he made his way down the line. A man was observed taking photos and people were shouting at him; he may have been a member of the press. Tempers flared with people when the man was even seen taking pictures of the bodies. A tragic reminder that there were young children on board was brought home to Ian when he saw various items like teddy bears on the track. The smell of diesel was in the air as he walked towards to level crossing with the other survivors.

* * * *

As soon as the train had stopped moving, guard Peter Sturdy climbed down onto the opposite rail line (the "down line") and shouted to the passengers to stay put while everything had settled. Looking around, he saw that all four carriages had left the rails, so climbing through the second carriage which was blocking the whole area, he ran back out the other side and down the track towards the oncoming 9.43 train from Beverley. He saw the train coming and waved his arms about to attract the attention of the driver, George Whitehead, who had seen the huge cloud of dust anyway and had started to commence stopping the train. It then went past Sturdy, braking heavily, before coming to a stand still. He ran back to the now stopped train and shouted to their guard Ray Waslin, to lay detonators to protect the rear of his train. Sturdy then ran back towards the crash site, and grabbed the phone at the crossing. The phone had a direct line to Beverley signal box, so immediately he told them what had happened and could they contact the emergency services. At this point he hung the phone up and noticed that the crossing alarm and lights were still operating. He headed back to the wrecked train to see if he could lend further assistance.

* * * *

The Thorpes in carriage four were starting to get their things together. At this moment they knew that the train had come off the rails as they were at a crazy angle, so they calmly took their luggage and started making their way out. Sliding the internal door to get to the back door, it slammed down on Brian's hand as all the weight was pushing it down. Leona had already hit her head on the window during the collision and the luggage had caused Gordon enough grief as it was. They got out of the carriage and looked down the line. It was now obvious that this was a major crash as they could see carriage one on its side and the first survivors climbing out. Looking down they saw a body and it hit home just how bad this was.

Turning back to the door, Brian lifted a pram to Gordon and manoeuvred it over the fencing; it was only upon looking inside that they realised there was a baby inside! Adrenaline kicking in had made the baby in the pram a lot lighter than it actually was. They took their luggage down and began making their way down the track to where the emergency services were already telling people to get to the crossing as quickly as they could.

Half-way to the crossing Gordon turned and looked at the scene. The upturned train and the remains of the van presented a shocking sight. Despite the slight injuries, they had been very lucky. Brian got stuck in with handing out cups of tea to people and making himself useful where he could. Until they could get out of the area what else could he do?

Darren White woke up in a strange place. Normally he would be staring at his bedroom walls after a sleep but this was different – he was outside and face down staring at dirt. He moved his head and was in pain, there was blood running down the left side of his face. As he realised he was lying in the middle of a dirt track he saw the train towering next to him. The suddenness of the realisation of what had happened hit him as he went into shock. A few people were walking around in a daze, he got up and walked over to the train where he saw Wayne lying on the floor as if he was asleep also. He stayed with him for a few moments, realizing that he could do nothing for his friend. He could see no immediate injuries but also no movement.

Darren had lost touch with reality as he figured out what had happened. His finger was badly cut and his backside was sore, with various cuts and grazes all over his body. He started staggering around. What should he do?

It now became apparent (although Darren may not have known this at the time) that he had been knocked unconscious against the window of the train. With the windows smashing, both he and Wayne had been thrown out of the train. He didn't realise that he was the only person who had been ejected from the window that would survive. He may have regained consciousness within seconds of the crash or it could have been up to ten minutes later, he didn't know. The dust cloud had settled by then and people had started getting out of the train. He started walking around in circles not really knowing what to do and not completely with it.

* * * *

Elva O'Brien stayed close to her family. At first it shocked them seeing somebody on the line, but soon realised it was people and that the train they were in wasn't even on the line any more. People were starting to jump out of the carriage and it was then they realised they too must get down on to the ground somehow. It seemed so high up – a lot different from boarding on a platform that's for sure. Elva jumped down with Lee and Maureen jumped with Adrian. Helen was petrified and couldn't jump down, especially with baby Jamie in her arms. Someone jumped up and grabbed Jamie which made her startled but she eventually got herself down onto the ground.

Walking on the gravel and grass they were very dizzy and unsteady on their feet. As Elva would describe it 24 years later: "It was as if you had just come off the Big Dipper at Blackpool."

Somebody was telling everyone to make their way to

the level crossing and head towards the two houses. They got themselves together and slowly started walking away from the train and towards the safety of the houses. It was now that she saw a young lad coming towards her. This was Darren White and he looked petrified. He was wandering around on his own and as they met up, Elva turned round and saw for the first time the carriage on its side. Nearby was Wayne Telling, lying on the floor next to the carriage with water dripping onto him. "That little lad is getting wet through," she thought and went over to him. She checked his pulse and immediately realised there was no sign of life. She pulled his jacket out of his hand and laid it over his face. To see he was dead came as a bit of a shock to her as he didn't look like he had a mark on him at that time.

Darren turned to Elva not long after and said: "That was my friend, we're gonna get into trouble, we're only going out for the day." This was obviously shock kicking in and he wasn't speaking or thinking straight. Over at the crossing cottages he sat there with the O'Brien's and kept looking down at the blood on his jeans and saying: "Look at my jeans . . . I think he's dead." With the reality not sinking in and after having serious concussion, his state of shock had Darren being more concerned about his jeans than of Wayne. (To this day he doesn't even remember meeting Elva).

* * * *

For Hilary Harbron, a gentleman gave her a hand helping her up and lifted her out of the train. Taking her down the track to the farmhouses, she sat on a wall and tried to come to terms with what had just happened. He turned to her and said that she shouldn't go to the other side of the train as that is where the most seriously injured people were. She had no idea that a woman had been thrown out of the window past her and had died. This would have been 73-year-old Joan Wilson who was on a shopping trip to Beverley with her sister Lorna Wilson. (Pure coincidence had it that Joan had married someone with the same surname as her, which caused the press to put Lorna Wilson down as her sister-in-law.) Hilary was allowed to use a phone in one of the houses and she rang her friend up to collect her. Because of the restrictions on entering the roadway, her friend Douglas had to park up and walk to collect her. As she seemed okay at this moment, she walked back with him.

Amanda West daren't move from her seat. Someone came up to her and guided her out of her seat, climbing down from the train and onto the track. Looking forward she saw the white houses and walked towards them. Looking over her shoulder she saw the wreckage of the train she had just come off. People were all over the place, climbing around the carriages, walking down the tracks. There were pieces of wreckage laid across the lines with handbags, shoes and other personal things. She dare not look too close in case she saw something that would haunt her for life. She looked back towards the crossing again and continued walking down looking straight ahead. She was shaking a lot and all she could think about was what could have happened to her had she been elsewhere on the train. If she had arrived earlier and got onto the first carriage. She was on her own again now, making way to the white houses, where people were already propped up against the wall.

It was here she met Christine Beckett who had her baby boy Craig with her in a pram. When the train began to sway, she said, she knew something was wrong and dove over her son to protect him. Glass had been flying around but amazingly she seemed uninjured. Amanda stood with her while she spoke to the press before realising that she needed to let her foster parents know. The Lunns were letting survivors and emergency services use their phone so she was allowed to ring them up and tell them what had happened. When she revealed that she had been in a train crash they were horrified. "Are you okay? Do you want us to pick you up?" came the concerned replies. But she declined the offer and just said that there was talk of a bus taking them away, she was not injured and would complete the journey to be picked up later.

* * * *

As he walked away from the area of the upturned first carriage, Jason Schofield could hear the engines going and noticed Richard Myerscough going to turn it off. The smell of diesel in the air was horrendous. As he headed to the crossing he saw people coming out of the houses. He slumped against the wall next to a bearded man who looked like he had broken his jaw. People were all over by this point trying to help the injured, checking those who were in shock. One woman came out of one of the houses with a cup of tea which he gladly accepted. It was cold but he didn't care, it gave him something to hold and bring a bit of moisture to his mouth.

Back at the crash site, Richard was busy with a large green first aid box that he had found, going to and from the site and the old station house, helping with the injured, which included broken bones and torn limbs. Survivors were being propped up next to the houses while they waited for the ambulances, which had started to arrive. His wife Marion was looking after the children as they were only young. Richard sent Stephen back to her but it wasn't long before he was soon back by his father's side. As they were going up the track they then noticed the bodies of those who had not survived. Thrown out of the train, they now lay next to the track as if they were asleep. Going back into the first carriage he found Joan Wilson in the toilet next to the luggage rack. She was black from head to toe and had been thrown into there by the force of the impact. Thankfully she was unconscious and apart from a loud bang, to this day, she remembers nothing about the initial collision. Bill Shaw had climbed in and was helping the driver Harry Brown get a bit more comfortable. The firemen then removed the front window and passed him out. He kept drifting in and out of consciousness and kept turning to guard Sturdy and muttering incoherently: "Are we still at Nafferton?"

Back on the track he then had to calm down Herbert Donnelly, who was frantic over the fact that although baby Jordan was fine – he didn't have a scratch on him – Annette was missing. Richard tried to grab him as he seemed in a bad way. "Calm down," he said. "Sit yourself down; wherever she is they will find her." But that was little comfort when your loved one is among the missing.

* * * *

Driving at top speed down the main road towards Driffield, Carol Dyson turned right down the country lane towards the wrecked train. She didn't look to see where the train was, she was concentrating on the road ahead, but within seconds it was plain to see that there was a major incident ahead. This wasn't just a car being hit by a train. She got to the two houses and parked up right outside them on the left-hand side, grabbed a little orange first aid kit and ran to the train. The kit was only the basic things like plasters etc, but it was better than nothing. As she got to the crossing the sight that hit her made her shocked. "Oh my God!" she thought as the wreck of the train and the staggering survivors greeted her.

Right behind Carol's car, PCs Sullivan and Holliday's car was by now approaching the crash site and in the distance they could see the carriages off the rails and sticking up out of the bushes and into the air. They, sped down towards the level crossing and pulled up. As expected, they were the first on scene and it was obviously a major crash with numerous people involved so Andy stayed by the car as the "anchorman" relaying information to and from the operations room by radio.

Bill got out of the car and the first thing he noticed was the crossing lights were flashing with the alarm still sounding. He made his way up towards the wrecked carriages and saw that someone had placed a canvas sheet over a body, although whoever was underneath was moving slightly. He saw the train's guard Peter Sturdy standing near the sheet shaking and staring into space. Sturdy had already done a lot to save the lives of the people on board and now he seemed to be visibly shocked.

By now Bill was running towards the train, trying to use his handheld radio to tell the ops room what was happening. Realising his radio didn't work and was nothing more than an expensive paperweight, he slammed it to the ground in temper. This really isn't the time for technology to fail on you! He saw people all over the place and they were heading into the field where the crops were pretty high. He was now trying to prevent people from going in there because if they were to succumb to injuries or shock and were to collapse then it would make finding them more difficult and it could cost them their lives. Noticing they are gone could take hours if they travelled alone, let alone finding them. He quickly surveyed the scene and decided to head back to Andy at the car.

Running back down the track, he went to the station house where people were already gathering. He asked if he could use the phone to ring the ops room up directly. He told them they required everything – police, fire, ambulance . . . "We want everything!"

* * * *

Pulling up shortly after Carol Dyson and not far behind the traffic police was Sergeant Ralphs. He could see the carriages as the car approached and knew that this was more serious than first thought. He saw the traffic policeman (Holliday) in the car pulled up and radioing back to the control room that there were "class 21 and class 22s" (Class 21s are deaths, 22s are serious injuries). As they had arrived Keith noticed that the crossing alarms were still activated and the first thing he thought was *I wish someone would switch that bloody noise off*. He then began the task of helping survivors down the track to safety.

Right behind them was PC Turrell's car. He was surprised at how few of the emergency services had turned up yet, but he parked on the side of the road on the grass verge about 100 yards from the crossing and made his way on foot. There were already a number of vehicles which had stopped soon after the crash so it was getting pretty crowded. He headed towards the wreckage and immediately saw the remains of Ashley's van on the side of the track and carried on towards the train. With a lovely hot sunny day, seeing this scene seemed very strange and surreal.

He saw that already people were making their way down the line, the walking wounded, the uninjured, the shocked. There seemed to be a steady stream of about half a dozen people at any one time. Others were still climbing out and giving a hand to those still trapped. At this point someone who obviously recognised him (although he couldn't place the face) walked past and said: "Dale, you need to get yourself over there . . . it's a right mess." To this day he does not know who he was or how he knew him, although at the time he most likely didn't take much notice of who it was, not with this disaster in front of him to sort out.

* * * *

Howard Brown had taken longest to get to the crash site having come from Brough, but still the work was only just beginning. He describes the scene over two decades later:

"As I walked towards the derailed carriages, there was a kind of surreal atmosphere hanging over the place: while there was desolation all around, the weather was beautiful and there was not a sound to be heard."

* * * *

Elva O'Brien heard someone shout out if that if anybody knew first aid to come back to the train and help out. Being a fully qualified care assistant, she volunteered to go back and see what help she could give. Walking back up the line she saw people hovering over someone on the line saying: "Joan, don't die!" and asking Elva if she could be saved. It was obvious that Joan Wilson was in a very bad way and would not survive, so she just said: "I'm sorry, I can't," but didn't tell them how bad she was as it was upsetting enough with her lying there. Further along she saw a man with head injuries, who she had seen running to get the train at Bridlington.

* * * *

By now a Lieutenant Colonel from the nearby army base had turned up and told PC Sullivan that they had a recovery wagon and, if he granted permission, would it be a good idea to clear the track and rip up what is left in order to get vehicles down there to aid rescue. They decided that yes, this was actually a good idea that could save time going into the fields and down the dirt road next to the line. However, the idea was put on hold when sirens were heard in the distance. There was now a fleet of blue lights heading towards the scene.

Bill then went back down to the carriages, seeing that people were staggering, crawling and using any means by which to reach safety. Some were very badly injured, so he helped whoever he could get them back down the track towards the houses where he had just come from. He sat them down in the flat areas between the two buildings and in the yards and it was at this point that he began taking names of the people there.

PC Holliday was still by his car relaying information live back to the ops room, doing the best he could in a very clear and very professional way. He became the primary means of contact between the police control and the scene of the crash.

By now many ordinary people were turning up to see if they could help in any way. Bill had comforted the injured the best he could, he now had to leave it to the ambulance crews to do their job. All the time he continued taking names. This would later prove to be a very good decision when questions were being asked.

* * * *

WPC Carol Dyson was by now guiding survivors down

towards the crossing. They seemed to be in a trance, like they were some kind of zombie, in a state of severe shock. These people had to be taken away as soon as possible, even if it was just away from the wreckage. Some didn't even look like they had any physical injuries. She made several journeys up and down the track where the other police took over and guided them away to the side of the houses.

As the Driffield fire-fighting team approached the scene, they could see the train from the road. It was only as they turned towards the crash site did they realised how big a job lay ahead. (If the scale of the disaster was known from the start there may have been more police/fire/ambulances sent away but the ambiguity of the information suggested that it was a small incident or a simple derailment with at the worst a few injuries.) As they came closer to the rail lines they saw walking wounded staggering away from the crossing. The engine turned right and parked in the field near where the police had already started setting up a base. They all got out and were met by other firemen already on the scene who told them that this was a major incident and that there were many fatalities.

Going straight to the carriages, their aim was to check to see if anyone was trapped alive and whether anyone needed to be cut out. Although it soon became apparent that there was nothing else left to do but simply to cut the remains of the dead out. The few trapped people (the young boy in the door and Mark Hullah with his arm) had already been seen to. Malcolm Gill was amazed at how big the train seemed. Because it was off the line and poking out into the field, it seemed so huge! The station officer said to them to not look around too much as there is rescue to be carried out on the other side, which is when they saw the upturned carriage. Looking around they then saw bodies and body parts laying amongst the wreckage.

A leading fireman grabbed Dave Smith and two others and directed them to spray a jet of water on a leaking fuel filler cap on the right-hand side of carriage two. This didn't take long as it soon ceased to leak and the area was damped down enough to not be a fire hazard.

The first job in any major incident was to conduct a quick survey of the scene, speak to people already there and find out what the situation was as it stood and it was then that they were told that people may be still trapped. Unless everyone could be accounted for they had to assume that people needed assistance in the worst case scenario. But it didn't take long before they realised that there was nobody left alive who could be rescued. Ladders were erected on the side of carriage one to allow easy access to the doors, which were now swung open. The only police officer to enter the carriage with the firemen at that point was Carol Dyson. She was more than relieved that she didn't have to do this on her own, that there were specialist teams here that could help her get into the coach and give assistance where possible. As she was lowered into the carriage, she looked around and noticed the amount of gravel that had littered around what was now the floor. The broken windows had scooped up copious amounts of stones and ballast. Looking to the rear, she saw Mary Foster lying half sitting up with her legs trapped covered in this gravel. She seemed to be alive and conscious, muttering incoherently and not making any sense. Mary did not have a clue what was going on, so Carol held her and rubbed her cheek, telling her that she was going to be all right, she was okay and that she would be out very soon. There was not only Mary in there; she saw the driver Harry Brown, passengers Mark Hullah, Simon Quinn and another, most likely Herbert Marsters who was still alive at that point.

As Malcolm Gill climbed the ladder to the driver's door, Barry Skelton entered in the open entrance of carriage one, having to shift pieces of wreckage out of the way. It was a bit awkward to work in a coach that was on its side, having to climb over seats and luggage racks, and everything else in between that had now fallen on to what was now the floor. He had to take his helmet off more or less straight away as it ended up getting in his way and causing a hindrance. He went straight to work and got his cutting equipment out, which actually only consisted of crowbars, hacksaws etc. Thanks to the coaches being very well built, this became a major problem trying to cut into the thick metal and wood. Their job now was to cut away to make doubly sure that no-one was alive under the train, and, if there were bodies, to be able to release them for recovery. Other fire-fighters came and cut the windows out of the driver's cab to get Harry Brown out, who was in a bad way but still alive. Others then put ladders up the side of the carriage so it provided easy access to the side doors on the "roof" to get people out. But the dread of only finding a few bodies was short-lived, for it became apparent that there were at least half a dozen dead. One body lay directly behind the driver and another had to be dug out via the window to get to it. Malcolm then noticed one of the windows still intact and to his horror a pair of feet underneath. This was obviously going to be a long task. A Beverley fireman went around carriages two, three and four to check inside and make sure they were clear, before everyone's concentration was on the upturned carriage one.

* * * *

It was about this time that, outside in the still hot sunny day, a rather bizarre incident occurred. Carol Dyson had taken her first aid kit from her car and had climbed into the first carriage to help with rescuing survivors too badly injured to move on their own. Although it was a policeman's job at that moment to secure the site and let the fire brigade and ambulance crews sort the victims out, she fearlessly entered the carriage with complete disregard for her own safety and was actually the only police officer to enter that carriage. She was doing the best she could in the situation, and in the commotion she had left her hat in her car and had also torn her uniform. On top of that she was covered in sweat, soot and grease from the wreckage. However, a senior police officer, Superintendent Douglas Taylor, who had not long been on the scene, decided it would be a good idea to remark about the fact that she should have had her hat on. It was decided that she should be sent away from the scene to make sure she was properly dressed. At a time like this, it provoked rage from several people who had to be held back from striking the man. Many people witnessed this and found it unbelievable that in the state she was in, there would be something so trivial brought up after all the hard work she was doing. Although in the end she dismissed the whole incident as if it never happened and, being a professional, she got straight back to work. It would later be said that the incident was purely an excuse to have her removed from the area in order for her to take a break from what she was doing. The fact that she was "removed from the area" only to return moments later was overlooked by the same people.

* * * *

A lot of ambulances were now on the scene and had started working their way round the walking wounded. Jason Schofield was in the first ambulance that left the scene. He had various injuries which included broken fingers and whiplash. He was put in the back of the ambulance with several others, crammed in near the back door sitting upright.

Marion Myerscough somehow ended up at Hull Royal Infirmary. Some of those who were taken to hospital were more injured than expected. One survivor was allowed to go home but ended up in intensive care in Leeds with suspected brain damage. For some reason Richard was on the list of victims and declared dead, although it is not known how anyone reached that conclusion as none of the Myerscoughs or Shaws were injured, and everyone had seen Richard working tirelessly to help people at the crash site. However, for some unknown reason, Richard had decided to walk away and hide under a hedge on the road towards Aike (today he still has no idea why he did this; it could have been exhaustion after the adrenaline-fuelled rescues caught up on him). His family went looking for him but it was one of the emergency services who found him and took him to hospital. He just turned to them and said that he wanted Stephen to go as well. They asked him what injuries he had sustained, as he had blood on his hands and shirt, although it was soon found that none of the blood was his.

* * * *

Local man Jim Bloom had been out that morning and was returning home when he saw the train from the road side. He raced home to the nearby village of Scorborough (not to be confused with Scarborough, a popular seaside town further up the coast) and went back up the track from the Decoy Farm crossing with his wife to lend assistance. They arrived maybe 20 minutes after the crash, with a cloud of dust still in the air. There were several emergency vehicles arriving by now. While he went to see if he could lend a hand up the track, his wife gave help to the Bayes and Lunns at the cottages, where survivors were gathering. Jim didn't enter the train and didn't want to get in the way of the emergency crews, but looking around he saw considerable devastation and a body lying on the side of the track.

* * * *

Barry Skelton and three others were still working hard in the upturned carriage. Other fire-fighters were there too; at some point there were around six or seven of them in there at any one time and maybe the odd ambulance man. Although it was a grim job, it seemed very calm in there as he started cutting the coach where they suspected that bodies were buried. It was very hot with the heat from the day and also the strenuous work that was being undertaken. He would be in the front coach for hours with his kit, cutting some of the seats away and some of the carriage side. But they all worked together as a team and got the job done, in the worst conditions possible, concentrating on the job in hand and not how bad a situation it was. It would be so easy to take a break and have a good cry, to weep for the devastation and of the lost loved ones. But that could wait, they had a job to do and the quicker they got it done the quicker they would be back outside. Dave Smith had to stay up top on the side of the carriage and he had a bird's-eye view of everything that was going on below. The crews were working closely with John Gosnold from the hospital to get the bodies out. The Beverley crews had rigged the ladders which made getting up and down a lot easier. Soon it was clear that nothing more could be done in carriage one, so they went onto the other carriages to see what else needed taking off.

It wasn't long before Dave's job was changed to passing messages to and from one of the senior officers, so his role was now to inform the control centre of what was happening and then relay any replies back to Assistant Divisional Officer Mitchell at the crash site. Directing the recovery operation from his position on the top of carriage one, he was later heard to remark about the carriages that "they don't build these carriages to be ripped apart easily," given the hard task of cutting through the sides.

* * * *

Bob Brown, who had pulled up in front of the houses, could see a lot of the people from the train were sitting in front of the two buildings. His job was to get these to the hospital as quickly as possible, although many more ambulances were now here and the field next to the track was full of fire-fighting vehicles, ambulances, police cars and even a huge tent. The army had turned up in the early afternoon and were giving out hot soup to the rescuers, who by now had been working nonstop for several hours in very difficult conditions. Also there to give help to them were the WRVS (Women's Royal Volunteer Service), who set up a stall to give out drinks to those still working. Although a relatively small contribution to the work in comparison, it made all the difference if you were running around trying to get a thousand tasks done as quickly as possible. Bob managed to get ten casualties and one fireman into his ambulance, even though there was actually only space for nine, and would take the more seriously wounded first. His job was to get people away as quickly as possible, which was easy enough when he literally found them all sat down waiting for him and promptly gathered them all up. A fireman with gashed leg, and a little girl sat on his knee in the cab, filled his quota and he raced to Hull Royal Infirmary. It didn't take long to get to Hull and when he arrived there somebody met them and six people with wheelchairs came and took them out of the back of the ambulance. First job done, his next task on the way back was to go to the HQ to pick up some body bags, 20 in all, which is all they had at that point. There was another 20 in another station and he knew where they were if he needed them. At this point in the day it was apparent that there were fatalities but no-one was sure exactly how many. They knew it was at least six, possibly a couple more trapped under the train.

* * * *

Photographer Terry Carrott was enjoying a relaxing weekend off at his home in Cottingham that morning, when a call came to him around mid-morning from the ever-vigilant freelance writer Tony Fairhurst. News of a train crash at Lockington, near Beverley was slowly filtering through . . . and there had been several deaths.

Terry immediately rang his news desk in Leeds to alert them – bearing in mind this was before mobile phones and he knew he would soon be on the road and out of touch with them.

Not being familiar with the rail layout in the area, like many others that day, he found himself in Lockington village itself. He parked up and took a long walk from the main Beverley road to the crash site at the level crossing.

Over two decades later Terry recalls the first images he saw. "A scene of utter devastation and one of those occasions when the professional adrenalin kicks in and you just get on with the job. I remember it being eerily quiet as the emergency services got on with their gruesome task of sifting painstakingly through the wreckage."

It wasn't long before he was joined by duty reporter Phil Ascough, from the Hull office of the *Yorkshire Post*, and freelance photographer Steve Morgan, who was covering the weekend for Terry anyway and had been tipped off by the *News of the World*.

Phil had been with the *Yorkshire Post* for three years and he was only by chance in the office looking to see if there was any mail to sort out. Normally there was no work on Saturday as there is not a Sunday edition of the *Post* (the only exception being the death of Princess Diana in 1997 when a special edition was printed). He was actually duty on-call reporter that weekend anyway, taking it in turn between two others, so he normally had two weekends off in three.

It was there that Steve Morgan had rung him, saying he had got word from the *News of the World* about this big train crash close by. If he had rung just minutes later he would have missed the call, but now he got straight on the phone to the head office in Leeds to tell them that he was going there straight away. He hung up, locked up the office and sped down Beverley Road.

It was only as he came to the crash site that he realised this was a major incident. Looking around he saw a line of ambulances racing to the site, but thankfully as it was on a country lane the traffic was very minimal. It would have been three times as chaotic if this had been on a major road. Although at this time less than an hour had passed, there was not a major road block in force, but priorities were given to emergency vehicles. He parked about a quarter of a mile away from the site so he wouldn't be in anybody's way and walked towards the level crossing.

He saw the field full of vehicles, the police not letting anyone else near the crash site and the WRVS had set a table up with drinks. He didn't even bother to get a drink; he would leave them for the guys who were doing all the work. They would need it later he was sure of it. Although he was keeping out of the way, he decided to start talking to people who were hanging around in that area.

Grabbing his camera, Terry started snapping photographs of the wreckage for the paper, although with it being a Saturday the *Yorkshire Post* would not be out until Monday. At this moment, because of the scale of the disaster, he made a decision to switch his standard black and white film for a colour one and began taking shots of the disaster in incredible colour clarity. It was a decision he would not regret.

Meanwhile Phil went to the nearest phone box to report what had gone on to the *Yorkshire Evening Post* who would hopefully run the story that night. He left the scene later that evening but planned to return the day after for a follow-up report.

* * * *

Over at the farmhouse, Bob and Mary Bayes were helping the survivors. They were keeping out of the way of the rescue workers so as not to hinder them but as they were walking down the track, Mary was making cups of tea for them and letting them sit in their house in different rooms. Survivors and rescue workers alike were recuperating in the kitchen, front room, yard…. One man in the yard spat his teeth out in the sink, others had very bad cuts and they knew that they needed hospital treatment. Bob and Mary were also letting the survivors ring their relatives to let them know what had happened. By now the police had contacted British Telecom to tell them what had happened and arranged for the line to be free of charge and open for them. Somebody else had organised a bus to come to the crash in order to collect people and take those who were not injured away from the crash site. Although they did have a brief conversation with the police, it didn't last long as they were very busy and still had plenty to be going on with.

* * * *

Postman Brian Mellonby was worried that the train crash that he had seen would have his daughter on board. She said earlier that she was thinking about going to Hull for the day and he immediately rang home where he then breathed a sigh of relief. His wife confirmed that she was not on the train. Reassured, he went up the line to render assistance and saw the bodies of the van driver and his foster son. Incredibly they were both alive; he even saw Malcolm's stomach moving. Although there were pieces of van around the track, it was not obvious that there had been a van involved, as the wreckage was just bits of twisted metal and pieces. He bent down to see if he could get any thing out of Malcolm Ashley, and asked if he was all right, but he was unconscious and no words were uttered back. He then apologised and said that he couldn't help as he did not know any first aid and didn't know what he was doing. He certainly didn't want to make someone worse trying to help them. He realised that there was nothing he could do and went back down towards a truck that had now pulled up. Speaking to driver Geoffrey Isles for a short while, it is then that WPC Dyson first turned up. He immediately told her about the unconscious bodies lying on the side of the track and not long after a fleet of blue flashing lights were heading down the street. With nothing more to do at this moment, he decided he would ring up Driffield post depot and explain what had happened. He said to them that there had been a major train crash and could he come back as he was pretty shaken up. However, they told him that he would have to carry on and complete the round. He then set off to deliver in Aike and then back through Beswick.

On the way to Scorborough, he stopped at Park Farm where a Mrs Taylor could tell something was amiss with him. Telling her about what he just witnessed, she gave him a brandy to calm down. He was visibly shaking and after spending about an hour at the crash site, was already late back to the depot anyway. Normally they had a quick cup of tea together, today he spent half an hour telling her what happened. And the great rush? Today was the day that everyone got their electricity bills.

* * * *

By now the road leading to the crash site had been cordoned off. More press had heard about the disaster and were appearing in their dozens. As soon as Ian Simpson got back to the crossing he was collared and photographed. He told the reporters what he had seen and what had gone on in the carriage; however, while he was doing this, his mother was close by frantic with worry but unable to get to him. It was only once they had finished firing questions at him did he realise that she was there ready to take him back home.

* * * *

Meanwhile back in Driffield, David and Jenny Carter were out in the garden shed packing and sorting things out ready for the house moving. A far away noise caught their attention. They heard sirens, not just one, but several. The first thought was that there must have been an accident on the Driffield by-pass, which wasn't unheard of, but it did happen now and again. Not long after they went back into the house and turned on the radio. The news came on and said that reports were coming in of a major train derailment in Humberside. This came as a devastating blow. Wayne was with Darren on a train travelling on that same line. Hopefully they are both OK and it was a different train. But a feeling of dread crept over them as very soon, their world would come crashing down in an instant.

* * * *

At exactly the same time a few doors down, Darren White's mother Pam was hanging washing out in the garden when she too heard the sirens, quite a few of them, more than normal. Like the Carters, she thought there had been a bad crash on Driffield by-pass and thought nothing else of it. Jenny rang her just moments later and said that she had heard on the radio there had been a train crash. "Put the radio on and listen," she said. The only problem was they didn't know which train it was or which direction it was going. Pam went straight to the radio and turned it on. The news reports were not frequent and she had to wait for the news on the hour bulletin to get any information. Keeping in touch with the Carters, somehow they found out that it was the train that Darren and Wayne were on. Their nightmare was only just beginning.

* * * *

Bill Sullivan's decision to take names at the crash site was now paying off. It started with just locals, villagers and anyone medically trained that were coming to lend a hand. Now it was families of the missing and injured that were heading towards the site. He had stayed away from the wrecked carriages for around three to four hours now, seeing various survivors like Ian Simpson and Len Robinson with their fingers cut up and bleeding from digging the young boy out of the gravel with nothing but bare hands and determination.

What made it that bit more personal, and frightening all the same, was that he thought his son Steven was on that train, *and* his daughter Deborah was planning to go to Hull that morning. On top of that so were his next door neighbours. It soon became apparent by the survivors, and looking around the train himself, that none of them had eventually gone out and by luck they were all safe and sound at home. It is only afterwards they realised what a good idea it was to have changed their minds at the last minute.

Now he was faced with worried relatives who were making their way down to the crash site. Thanks to him taking the names down, he was at least able to partially confirm or deny that they had survived. He knew some of the people who were coming to see him, friends of friends, people who he saw in the street on a daily basis. He would console those who came to inquire, who were obviously distraught, and gave what details out that he could, making notes of names that were missing in case anyone else could give him further information at a later hour. Among those he saw was Herbert Donnelly, still in a lot of shock and still looking for Annette. Again, she was not on Bill's list.

At this point he was made aware that the Chief Constable was arriving with a local MP, at which they were directed to see Bill Sullivan, with him being the first on the scene. The MP began asking him questions to which he replied that he could and would not divulge that information to him, he was on duty and the only person who he would talk about the crash to was the Chief. He ran through everything that had happened and how he had handled the situation.

Carol Dyson had been up on patrol since 7am and had been at the scene of the crash all day when the helicopter came around. Somebody told her that if she wanted it was okay now to leave the area and go back, but this time go out in the helicopter. After a day like this she could have done with getting away and having something exciting to do. She had witnessed death and misery all day and the thought of leaving by air was actually quite a good thought. But alas, the person in charge of her would not allow it and she would return back by car.

It hadn't been easy for her, she had seen heart-rending scenes all day like Herbert Donnelly walking around saying: "My wife, I can't find my wife…she's pregnant and I can't find her."

There was nothing she could do for him except tell him to go back down towards the crossing and wait with everybody else. She would learn later that his fiancé Annette did not survive the crash.

The helicopter's view from overhead.

Close up taken from the helicopter.

Yorkshire Post photographer Terry Carrott captures the remains
of the van with the train in the background.

Emergency services take over the field next to the crash site.

Emergency crews swarm the overturned first carriage.
Note the ladders placed there by fire crews.

Police Officer Sgt Keith Ralphs at the crash
(foreground with fluorescent jacket).

PC Dale Turrell kneeling down at the side of the wreckage.

Police officers walking back towards the crossing.

Police and fire crews working together on carriage one.

Evidence is passed to other police officers for examination.

Carriage one now propped up on blocks. You can clearly see inside the carriage where the carnage took place.

Fire crews survey the scene.

The remains of Malcolm Ashley's van GWX 475T
on the side of the track - one of five pieces.

Left: A distressed Herbert Donnelly
holds baby Jordan while being
comforted by a stranger.

Below: Beverley fire fighters take a
break. Barry Smithson is sitting down
with no helmet.

Long after the rescues had taken place, the police and fire
services still had jobs to do.

Exhausted fire crews take a break in the main field while others take
over on the carriages.

An overhead shot showing how far the train wreckage travelled from the initial
impact at the crossing. Note the police Portakabin outside the station house.

Overhead view showing the station house and how far away the train came to rest following the collision.

Damage to carriages two and three, while the first carriage remains on its side.

This photo shows the door that rescuers had to squeeze through to get to passengers, which was harder than it looks from this angle.

Police and fire crews discuss their next steps once there were no more people to rescue.

Carriage two across both sets of tracks. Guard Peter Sturdy ran in through one door and out of the other to get to the oncoming train from Beverley.

A collection of photos showing the various stages of removing the wreckage over the few days following the crash. The line would be reopened in just four days.

Chapter 4

Searching for the missing

Chaz Walker was still on watch at Hutton Cranswick station. He was getting phone calls from all kinds of people, but he was mainly taking updates on the crash from Beverley. It was only about an hour after the initial crash that he realised how bad it was. From what he could gather, the train from Beverley had seen a huge cloud of dust and managed to stop in plenty of time. Using the telephone at a nearby farm crossing they rang and let them know. Luckily they didn't get close enough to the site, although even if they did they would have run over detonators that the Peter Sturdy had already laid straight after the crash.

Although he was trained in what to do in an emergency, it still came as a shock and he still ran through a mental check list a hundred times or more to make sure that he was doing everything that he was supposed to do and not missing anything out. But he realised soon enough that he had done all he could. The only thing he had to deal with now was people coming up to him asking him why the trains were not running. He would just tell them to take the bus as he had no idea when the line would re-open or when they would start running the trains again. Normally Chaz was supposed to finish at 2pm that day, but the afternoon watchman always had other jobs to do and took over at 1pm every day. Chaz gave him his hand-over and informed him of the situation before heading straight home. It was only when he put the TV on and saw the first images of the crash on the news that he realised how much of a mess it was.

* * * *

Working as a switchboard operator in Hull that day was Lorraine Beasley. She had been informed of the crash down the line and was slowly getting information in about the details of the disaster. It was during this shift that she got a phone call from her mother. The Quinn/Marsters family were close relations and had been on that train returning from their holiday in Bridlington. Lorraine's father was due to pick them up and the train hadn't shown up. It was only when news filtered through about a train crash that they realised it was them. She quickly rang the incident helpline that had been set up and gave all the details she could about the six people. What was then unexpected and pretty shocking was the fact that the policeman on the other end of the line was asking very strange questions. Do they have any distinguishing marks on their bodies? Do any of them have false teeth? A feeling of dread crept over her. The only thing they promised was that they would check everything out and let them know as soon as they could. By 6pm that night her shift had finished and she had got no further news.

* * * *

By now people were arriving at Hull Royal Infirmary by the van load. Richard Myerscough arrived by ambulance with a load of people he didn't know, and the first thing he noticed was how loud the siren was. He asked if it could be turned off as it was now starting to become annoying. He was surprised when in the hospital a man approached and asked for him by name. Speaking to him he said that everybody was talking about him and had heard about the work he had done at the crash site. But thanks to his work there, he was minus his jacket; somehow he had lost it in the train somewhere with all his credit cards in. The hospital was full of the injured off the train and nearby a vicar was seen to be leading a very distraught family away, while another very distressed woman was screaming out a loved one's name as she came through the door.

* * * *

Back at the train crash site, there was no more rescuing to be done. The survivors had all been taken away, and most of the missing had been located. There appeared to be six bodies around the train, but until the first carriage was lifted they would assume there was at least one other underneath. The priority now had changed from rescue to recovery. The fire-fighters took video footage of the scene and worked with the ambulance men to help in the finding of the bodies. It was the police officers' job to stand guard on the bodies when they were found. The senior police officers assigned one PC to each body to act as coroner's officer, and Keith Ralphs was in charge of those PCs. The body bags were brought in and were guarded by the same officers. WPC Dyson left the scene in an ambulance to the mortuary, where she handed over the body of a male to the teams waiting there.

The Army School of Mechanical Transport at Leconfield had turned up with some heavy lifting equipment to help lift up the carriage, but their vehicle wasn't strong enough and couldn't lift it. The coach was made stable by supporting it with wooden blocks.

As the bodies were recovered and placed in bags one by one, they were taken away in the back of Bob Brown's ambulance, each one having its assigned police escort until they were turned over to the mortuary at Hull Kingston General.

At this point there was a one-way system set up

around the site with the road blocked so no-one except emergency vehicles could get through. Keith told a PC to go back to the crossroads and not to let anyone down unless they are official. (It was only hours later that he found out that he wouldn't let down Father Michael Murray, a local priest, who wanted to pray for the dead.)

Normally the fire officer is the incident officer and would dictate what could be moved as the investigations were going on. Things would be marked like personal items, bodies, etc., and were photographed by scenes of crime police and the firemen. It was a good few hours before they could start moving the bodies. Bob Brown collected the first three with three police escorting and went off down the road.

* * * *

Elva O'Brien had seen many a sight already, now she was watching the ambulance crews working on Wayne Harman down the track. She made her way back to the houses where it seemed the woman there was constantly boiling the kettle! "She was absolutely brilliant, I don't know how she managed," she would recall later. Also present by now were officials from British Rail, who started asking around to see what the immediate cause of the crash was. Was there anything or anyone on the line? But she replied that she had been sitting down and didn't see anything. Not long after came a press reporter, who, by Elva and a few others, was simply told to "Bugger off."

* * * *

For PC Bill Sullivan time didn't even come into the equation that day. He had worked hard from the moment he arrived at the scene and carried on doing his duty up until Chief Constable David Hall took him to one side and dragged him over to the WRVS stand. He sat him down and said to the woman serving: "Give him a cup of tea." That moment was the first time he had taken a moment out to recuperate. If it had been left to him he would have probably collapsed with exhaustion, there was work to do and he didn't want to stop until the job was done.

British Rail officials were now here, along with the British Transport police and the press all asking him the same questions. Were the lights working? Were the sirens working? On top of that he had Superintendent Taylor to contend with. He had told him about the list he had made of the passengers and what he had been doing on scene. Taylor would now take over the site from the uniform side and the investigations would begin.

Sullivan would stay at the scene until around 5pm or 6pm in the evening, having done all he could. It was now up to the team of investigators, although he would return to the crash site very soon to guard the wreckage.

* * * *

The grimmest task of the day was trying to recover the severed limbs under the train. It became apparent that they just had to be collected together and placed in three separate bags for the mortuary to sort out. This was neither the time nor the place to start piecing limbs together like some horrendous jigsaw. The Chief Constable turned to Keith and just said: "We're having a bad day, aren't we, Sarge?"

Dale Turrell made at least two trips to Kingston General Hospital in ambulances with the bodies. He helped in the recovery and loading them into the back of the ambulances, each trip taking about and hour and half. Nearby a surgeon was seen to arrive in full operating gear asking if anyone needed any amputation to free them. When he was told that all those here were dead, he went straight back to Hull Royal. Another surgeon, Dr John Gosnold, also from Hull Royal, would be in carriage one helping extract Herbert Marsters and Mark Hullah before giving assistance with the recovery of the more unfortunate ones who had not survived.

As the bodies were arriving in Kingston General, the ambulance would be backed up and the dead wheeled out before setting off again back to the crash. Bob Brown would make three journeys with the dead, and a further one to Hull Royal to pick up more medical supplies.

Howard Brown was also looking after bodies.

Wearing a yellow reflective waistcoat, he noticed that they were attracting hundreds of thunderbugs. Dotting around his clothes in the heat, it was just one more of an annoyance, together with the sweat running down their faces and the fact that they still had a lot more tasks that they were all faced with. Howard was given "his" body to look after, to which it wasn't actually revealed who or what was in the bag until it was unzipped at the mortuary.

* * * *

Also turning up that day to recover wreckage was local garage owner Bill Fussey. He saw the attempt by the army to lift the carriage and was told that there was a steam-powered crane coming all the way from Wales to do the job. However, his task was to recover what remained of Ashley's van. He owned a flat-bed truck and the police wanted the wreckage moved to Beverley for forensic examination. It was found that the van was still in second gear, quite normal for a car that was just setting off.

Bill had earlier been stopped by the police asking which way the train line was, to which he directed them across the main road – an easy mistake to make if you didn't know the area. After all, the signs point that way to Lockington and there are no signs to say that the railway lines are any different.

* * * *

When a red double decker bus offered the uninjured survivors a trip to Beverley, Amanda West got on it to complete her journey, meeting her friends as planned, although now under different circumstances. Beverley was closer than Bridlington and her friends only lived round the corner from where the bus dropped them off. The whole bus ride she sat downstairs next to the emergency exit. She was still very much in shock but stayed with them until her foster father picked her up that evening.

* * * *

As the rescuers worked tirelessly through the day and into the evening, it became apparent that there were six people killed in the crash. Some bodies would take longer than others to identify. Joan Wilson and Herbert Marsters died in Hull Royal Infirmary not long after arriving. The disaster took its final, ninth victim that night when Wayne Harman died in hospital of his injuries just after 9pm, his mother by his bedside. He had never regained consciousness following the crash and had been on a life support machine the whole time. Malcolm Ashley was still in critical condition and would not be told the details of the crash for a while. There were still ten more in hospital who would remain there for several more days.

Also in hospital joining the survivors at hospital

would be two firemen, one who would be treated for a cut finger and the other an injured knee, both sustained in the rescue operation.

* * * *

At some point with the emergency number in force (based at Scunthorpe) , someone had rung in and said that their daughter was on the train, a little girl. The train and fields were searched before they rang back to confirm that she was safe and well and didn't go on that train. For some reason, in the confusion, this had not got through to the ambulance staff on site but *had* with the police. The chief ambulance officer was not happy at not being told that they were no longer looking for a potential survivor/fatality.

* * * *

The rescue operation officially ceased at around 5pm and Bob Brown left his ambulance and went to get some pot mess from the army tent. This was the first time he'd eaten in hours, although he didn't realise this at the time. There was food and drinks on site and had been there the whole time, but up until now he had always been busy. In the end a man put a plate to him and just said "eat that" and only then he realised how hungry he was. It was the first food he had had since 8am that morning.

Dale Turrell could now relax a little more and had a

cup of tea at the WRVS stall. More and more people were slowly heading off now, although the press were still hanging around wanting the latest, a helicopter even hovering around and landing in a nearby field. One by one the ambulances, fire engines, police cars and others would go home.

Coming back from work that evening was Phillip Crossland. He was working in Hull and returning on a bus. As he was passing the crash site, he could see from the main road a lot of commotion and wondered what was going on. At first he thought there had been a tractor accident but the amount of police and ambulances, he knew that it must be something a lot bigger. From a distance he could make out the roof of the train at a funny angle and he said to himself: "Oh, it's a rail crash." The bus then went on its way and they passed the site. What he was not to know is that his old friend Harry Brown was the driver.

* * * *

Jason Schofield's ambulance ride to Hull didn't even register in his mind. He came round naked in a room surrounded by nurses and doctors and was told he had been in a train crash. He was kind of in and out of touch with reality due to the shock. He must have been suffering from memory loss because he kept asking about Greg, but no-one there had told him the truth yet and wouldn't do for a long time to prevent him from going back into shock.

His mother and sister came to the hospital at some point once they had found out about it. Jason's friend had heard the news and rung them straight away and said that Jason and Greg had been on a train and that a train had now crashed. He was pleased to see them but all they could do was ask how Greg was. He wasn't ready to hear the truth yet.

It was the day after the crash when a doctor and padre pulled the curtain round and held his hand, told him that he was going to be ok, but that Greg had died at the scene. He was crying non-stop and was in considerable distress for a very long time. The vicar stayed with him by the bedside for a long while after.

Jason was in hospital only a few nights, but because of the shock of both the crash and losing Greg, all the pain from his injuries didn't come out for a while. He went home with his fingers taped up and bandaged, wearing a neck brace. He remembers people at the hospital being asked by the newspapers if they wanted to talk about the crash. Jason was in the papers as being a survivor including a photo of him sat on the settee at home. But he was not wishing to talk to anyone right now.

* * * *

Mary Foster remembered nothing. Sitting by herself on

the train, she heard a bang and the next thing she knew she woke up in Hull Royal Infirmary. Her daughter Julia, who lived in Scarborough at the time, had come over to Bridlington to see her father Fred. When she had arrived he had said to her: "I can't stop long, I have to meet your mother off the train."

Julia suddenly had a feeling and said: "Mum has been in an accident"

Fred, wondering where that sudden comment had just come from, simply said: "Is she ok?"

She said that she didn't know and she had no idea how she knew this. She then took Fred to the hospital. Waking up out of unconsciousness in the late afternoon after the crash, Mary was in quite a lot of pain with injuries which included a broken jaw, broken finger and badly damaged legs. To this day she has never been right in herself because of this. Mary would remain in hospital for only a few days, but couldn't eat anything due to her broken jaw. Fred would have to liquidise her food for her for a while.

* * * *

Trevor Wilson and his wife Maureen were busy on that Saturday. It was market day in Bridlington and on top of running their sweet stall, their daughter Sarah needed collecting from Sheffield earlier on and he used a van that he had borrowed to travel all the way there, drop her off at home and then head back to the market where he would grab some lunch. Although it was a baking hot day, he went and got a jacket potato. While he was away, various people were chit-chatting about a bad accident near Beverley. There had been a train crash of some kind was what Maureen could make out. A bad one too!

Suddenly two police officers appeared at the stall and her first reaction was "What's he done this time?" although Trevor was only getting his spud! They said that they had to speak to Trevor about an important matter and would wait for him. Thinking he was in trouble of some kind for some unknown reason, she began thinking of what could have gone on that required two officers to talk to him. Everything became clear when Trevor returned and was taken to one side and told that his mother and auntie were involved in a train crash. News had been filtering through to the public on the radio but with all sorts of general gossip you didn't know what to believe.

Questions were going all over his head. Are Joan and Lorna OK? How bad is it? Where were they going on the train? The police gave Trevor a lift back home where Sarah was still waiting, wondering why her father was being escorted by the police. It soon became apparent that it was bad news. Joan had been fatally injured in the crash and his auntie Lorna was injured in hospital. He would have to formally identify Joan's body when he had the chance to compose himself and take it all in. He was very shocked and distressed. Maureen had to sort the stall out in the market, while Trevor rang round his family to break the news to them. He first called Richard, then David, all of whom were in a state of shock at the suddenness of it all.

* * * *

Lorraine Beasley finished work from the switchboard in Hull and headed home. She immediately phoned her mother to find out if there was any news. It was then she was told that Elsie and Herbert Marsters and Christine Quinn were among the dead. Christine's husband Peter and their two children Claire and Simon were injured and in hospital, although they were out of danger. Having worked with the railway company and finding out about the crash first hand, it made the news all the more devastating to her.

* * * *

The parents of Annette Stork had not known about the plans to go to Hull that day. It was when she went for fish and chips down the road that Christine Stork was first told that there had been a bad train accident. She remarked that it sounded awful, but thought no more about it, concentrating more on getting home while the chips were still hot. After they had eaten, Christine,

Melvin, Julie (Annette's sister) and four-year-old Michelle (Julie's daughter) planned on going to Nafferton to pick strawberries. But when they sat down to eat, the phone rang. It was Herbi and he was not in a good way. He told them basically that they had been involved in the train crash and couldn't find Annette. He and Jordan were fine physically and could they come to Hull Royal to pick them up?

Shocked at what they were now hearing, they raced off to Hull in the middle of the afternoon where they saw Herbi in the hospital in a bad way. The only distress Jordan was in was due to the fact he had lost his dummy somewhere. Luckily he didn't have a mark on him.

All they could do now was wait and see what happened, hopingAnnette had wandered off or been picked up by another ambulance and taken elsewhere. But things were not looking good when the police started calling. They started asking what jewellery she was wearing, which they replied she had a signet ring which was very significant in design. Soon the dreadful news they were all hoping wasn't true came to light. Annette was one of the victims.

* * * *

June Sturdy was working that morning and when it came to dinner time, she went out on her lunch hour into Hull and immediately saw newspaper placards which said there had been a major train crash. She went back to work and rang up the Hull depot who said that her husband, train guard Peter Sturdy, was in the crash but he was OK. Although she was concerned she carried on at work, safe in the knowledge that Peter was all right and she would see him later. Returning to home at around 5.30, she saw that Peter was already there and was sitting in one of the living room chairs. He didn't say much, only that he had been in the crash and that some people had been killed. It was only when it came on the news and he began to get upset did she realise how bad it was.

* * * *

Detective Sergeant Colin Andrews was on duty doing normal CID cover. He had got a phone call from one of the detective inspectors within about half hour of the crash. They asked him: "Could you go to Lockington as there has been a train crash?" He had to travel from Goole to Lockington, which took around an hour, arriving on scene around mid-morning. He pulled up on the side of the road and saw the devastation for himself. By this time the rescue was now a recovery mission and his initial job was to do the inquiries. The first was to prioritise what tasks needed doing – preserving the forensic evidence, identify the bodies, contact any relatives. Getting straight to work, he would stay at the scene for the rest of the day.

* * * *

WPC Dyson returned to Beverley Police station once she had finished at the mortuary. The first thing she had to do was to submit a formal report, which she did straight away. Being both mentally and physically exhausted, she went home to an empty house. Picking her phone up, she called her mother to tell her what had happened; she had to talk to someone about this or she would break down. Once she had poured out all the details, she hung up, went upstairs and ran herself a hot bath.

* * * *

Following the realisation that there had been a crash, it soon became obvious that it was Wayne and Darren's train that had been involved. Racing around, the Whites and Carters were heading to the hospital to find out more information.

At around mid-day, Pam's husband Rick, together with their 15-year-old daughter Linda, took the car and drove down to Aike to see the crash for themselves; it seemed pointless just hanging around doing nothing. They saw the police cordons at the crossing, but they wouldn't let them through. However, a deal was made that if they took a member of the press down then they would be classed as official and would be allowed to go down. This they did and they came across a police officer who knew Darren through being at Scouts. He told them that Darren was one of the survivors and he had seen him being taken away to the hospital alive and safe. They thanked him and headed back to Pam and the Carters with the news. At the same time, Pam had already got a phone call from Hull Royal saying that Darren was there and his injuries were not critical. He was OK for now but would have to be kept in hospital overnight. Straight away they got back on the road to Hull and headed for the hospital.

Darren was found by Pam and Jenny and he was instantly overjoyed. He was now no longer on his own. They saw that he was injured with a cut to the right side of his forehead next to his eye which needed 13 stitches, part of his finger was flapping about and he had various other internal injuries, although no-one seemed to know where Wayne was. Could he have been taken to a different hospital? Is he injured? Could he be in this hospital but no-one knows who he is? All kinds of questions were running around but as usual in situations like this, there are always very few answers. With David remaining at home in case of any phone calls, Pam didn't want to leave Jenny on her own in the hospital to go and see Darren as she would be on her own. In a bid to figure out where Wayne was, a policewoman came to see Darren to ask about the last time he had seen him.

Although a helpline had been set up for worried relatives, no-one seemed to be able to get through to anyone. On the radio it said that everyone was accounted for, but still no-one knew where Wayne was, and it was getting very worrying.

It was decided that they should head back home. If Wayne wasn't here then there is no point in hanging around. Going back, there were heading towards Lockington and they asked the driver to take a different direction away from Lockington, which he did. Getting back home there was still no news, so David had the number of a senior police officer, which he rang. Faced with a distraught parent, the man on the other end of the phone gave it to him unofficially but straight: "I shouldn't be telling you this . . . but . . ."

Wayne Telling was dead. They would soon be getting a visit to tell them officially, which happened not long after. David and Jenny went to pieces. Everything that was planned for the family over the past few years had suddenly been torn apart. By this time Pam and Rick had gone back to the hospital to see Darren again, so they rang Pam's mother and left a message. There was nothing more they could do.

* * * *

A friend came to the hospital to pick up Richard and Stephen Myerscough and decided to go the Driffield road way so they could see the crash site again but in a clearer setting. As they come up to the cross roads, they saw the train, and up until now they didn't realise that it wasn't level, and that it was kind of "stacked up" in the air. It looked so strange, knowing that they had come off that just hours earlier. Meanwhile, Marion and David went home from the crash site by bus, although there were no arrangements made to get people home from the hospital. It was all left for the relatives of the survivors.

* * * *

Hilary Harbron arrived in Hull to collect her car and amazingly managed to drive it to Cottingham. Only when she sat down to listen to the radio did she realise how bad the crash had been. She had not given her name to any of the reporters at the houses and although she doesn't remember giving her details to the police, there were two officers round to see her later that afternoon when she had driven back home. Sue Dales remembered nothing. She woke up in hospital vaguely and for just seconds in the X-ray department before slipping back into unconsciousness. It was a while later that she woke up fully in the ward. She didn't have any major injuries, only slight cuts and a lump in her back where parts of her spine had compressed. At some point she was told what had happened but does not remember how or when to this day. The day was a bit of a blur to her, never realising how close she had been to going under the train and joining Greg Addison. She was one of the luckiest survivors in carriage one to make it out alive and to not have any mental scars or trauma. It was almost like she had never been there compared to, say, Jason Schofield who had seen everything from start to finish.

* * * *

For the emergency services, they were now winding down after a very hard day. All the survivors were in hospital, all the dead had been taken away to be identified. Now the manpower and the tasks were being scaled down and personnel were being released to go home.

Barry Skelton, Malcolm Gill, Dave Smith and the rest of their fire crew set off back to the station at around 1430 when they were told that they were no longer needed at the scene. They went out as a team of six and came back as a team of six, never getting split up no matter what. The only time Dave saw Barry a bit "rattled" was when he thought for a brief time that his daughter had been on the train, which was later confirmed that she hadn't. The only thing left to do for them was to get the gear cleaned up and prepped ready for the next call out.

When the ambulances were no longer needed, they too were sent back, keeping one ambulance on stand by at the scene with driver Tony Capes in case the people still working in the wreckage needed it. Bob Brown took his ambulance back to the depot in Driffield where he parked up and left it. It didn't need a clean as incredibly, after all that, it wasn't even that dirty. So he rang home and spoke to his wife Edith, asking her to come and pick him up. After a long day with countless journeys to and from the crash site and various hospitals, he eventually got home just after 8pm that night. Edith had been out shopping as planned but on her own. It was only when she saw the news that night did she realise how bad it had been. Bob took his clothes off, filled up the bath and relaxed; he didn't want to even think about Lockington any more. He had already had five Christmases in a row ruined by young boys being killed on the road a few years back. (He would not talk about the crash again for 23 years until I interviewed him for this book.)

A police incident room was set up in the shape of a portacabin outside the old Station House. There the investigation would be coordinated, with the locals making them refreshments through the coming days. Sergeant Keith Ralphs went back to Beverley station and wrote some quick notes on the crash in his office. He went home at around 6pm. That night he went to the police club for some drinks. He definitely needed them today.

* * * *

Elva O'Brien was placed in an ambulance with her family and she noticed a young man with a baby getting on too. This was Herbert Donnelly with his year-old baby Jordan; he looked very distraught and absolutely terrified. He didn't speak the whole time, even when they eventually got to the hospital and were sat down at tables. Jordan had a slight bump on his head but was otherwise fine. Annette was still missing; by now she was believed to be dead.

Not long after, Elva went in to get an X-ray as she had suffered whiplash in the jerking of the train and a slight knock on her head, although at the time she didn't realise. Luckily she was the only member of her family to have even a slight injury. The praise from the O'Brien family that day were for the nurses. "They were brilliant. The staff in the hospital want a gold medal. Tea for everyone, smoke if you wanted to, toys for the kids, nappies for the babies, tins of biscuits, the nurses really put themselves out that day."

Then they were greeted by men from British Rail who asked them where they were going. They then arranged for two taxis to take them all the way back to Barnsley and they eventually arrived home at around 5.30 that evening. It still didn't really hit them just how big the crash was and how much of an effect it would have on them all until that night when she was playing with little Jamie in front of the fire. After he had had a sleep on Helen's lap and being given something to eat, he would always like to play with a shoe box full of toy cars, tractors and lorries. He lined them all up and sat back, just looking at them. A car transporter was brought out of the box and one of them was making car noises, but he pushed it away and said: "No, No!"

"Don't you want to play?" said Elva. He shook his head: "No….no," to which he pointed at the transporter and simply said: "Fall down, fall down!"

He never played with his cars again. He knew that train had gone over and it had clearly had an effect on him.

* * * *

For PC Dale Turrell, he had spent a while at the crash and eventually left at around 6pm to 7 pm, going back home to Hessle where his wife was waiting. Other than people at the scene of the crash, he had not discussed this with anyone else. He hadn't been in long when the phone rang. Iit was his father asking if he had seen the train crash on the news. "Dad, I've been there all day pulling victims out."

At that moment he was given the news that his cousin Annette Stork was on the train and had not survived. He had seen all the victims except the two that were trapped under the train and it suddenly hit him who one of them now was. Although they were close as children, by the time he had joined the police he lost touch with most family members but now and again still saw them around. Today had come as a bigger blow than just attending a train crash.

* * * *

The press had been there most of the day too, from the national newspapers and ITN news to local reporters and Radio Humberside. Basil Lewis was out that day to cover the half marathon near Pocklington for the *Saturday Morning* program and had got as far as Shiptonthorpe when a call came in saying that there had been a train crash. The team in the van slowed down and waited until more details came in and very soon were told to head towards Lockington as it now seemed that there had been a major incident. Their main job was to get information and provide communications between the crash site and the studio. It was around half an hour after the crash and they were the first media on scene with them being in the area anyway.

As they approached the turn off towards the level crossing from the main road, the police were stopping everyone from going down that way except emergency services, and from where they were parked they could just about see the crash site. The only thing they could report on at the time was how many ambulances, fire engines and police cars were going to and from the scene. No details could be given that were precise so they reported what they could, listening to police conversations over the radio for any further details.

Meanwhile at his home, a senior breakfast presenter from BBC Radio Humberside was listening to the radio and heard the first reports. He called the radio station and offered any help that would be needed.

After a while, the team was allowed down to the farm at the level crossing where they could see more of the disaster, and it was here that a female member of the team decided she didn't want to do the report as she was uncomfortable being there, so she was allowed to go on her way.

It was only later in the day that they were allowed down to the crash site to view the train crash for themselves close up. Until then there had been a police PR officer giving all the reporters what they could and that in turn was sent off to their HQ. They were allowed to park their broadcast van in the field as long as they stayed out of the way of the emergency workers still trying to do their job. Ian Cundall from BBC Television was being filmed at the site for the news bulletins.

At around 4pm they left the scene of the crash, with nothing more to report other than it was now closed off for investigators to begin the task of trying to establish a cause of the disaster.

* * * *

Harry Brown, the train driver, had two breaks in his leg, three broken ribs, head injuries and several internal injuries. He drifted in and out of consciousness for a long time, his wife by his side the whole time. He would later leave hospital, being the last survivor to leave hospital, but would never be well enough to go back on to trains.

Having never got over the Lockington crash, he died four years later.

* * * *

At the police station in Hessle an incident room was set up, with several detectives now in on the inquiry. A huge diagram of the train layout was on the wall showing who sat where at the time of the collision. Detective Superintendent Barry Lilley was in overall command in the incident room co-ordinating the investigation, and now the rescue was over, questions needed to be asked. Why did Malcolm Ashley's van end up on the railway line? Were the warning lights working correctly? Did the sirens sound? Was the train driver at fault? One rumour even circulated that 11-year-old Wayne was at the wheel of the van! Despite it being highly unlikely, every angle had to be looked at and eliminated.

Colin Andrews left the scene of the crash in the evening and drove back to Hessle police station. He was given the job of assisting the outside investigators and supervising the teams that were going out but working from the incident room. The investigation had only just started and would take a long time to gather all the relevant information.

* * * *

That Saturday night, photographer Terry Carrott got a

phone call from Chris Bye, the deputy editor of the *Yorkshire Post*. He wanted to know about the photographs he had taken at the scene and whether he had done any colour shots. At the time it was early experimental days of the use of colour photos in newspapers and very expensive in the process. However, he replied that he had got some excellent images of the disaster in full colour. With that, it was decided there and then that his his colour photos would be on the front page of Monday's *Yorkshire Post*.

Phil Ascough returned as planned on the Sunday, the day after the crash. He had various contacts in Driffield itself and had kept in touch with what the investigators and police were doing. His reports were like Terry's photographs – front page.

* * * *

It was the Sunday newspapers that first alerted Barrie Harman to the Lockington disaster. Reading the stories of the crash he was shocked to see the name Wayne Meinke printed. Was this his son? He immediately rang members of his family who had actually been trying to get in touch with him all day. Heartbroken Barrie knew there was nothing he could do. He placed a small notice in the newspaper commemorating his boy and attended the funeral.

Today he has no ill feelings towards his ex-wife Ethel,

who died not so long after losing her fight with alcoholism. He has since moved on with his life and refuses to get angry about what might have been. Both Ethel and Wayne are no longer here, no-one to defend themselves in an argument, no-one to answer the unanswered. He looks ahead in life but remembers Wayne with a fondness that only a father can, on birthdays and obviously in every July since his death. He even works alongside a survivor of the crash today and has done for several years, now and again talking about it whenever something crops up.

* * * *

Trevor and Richard Wilson, still very shocked by the events that had unfolded, went to see their auntie Lorna in Hull Royal Infirmary where she lay with a broken arm. She was in a bad way at this time and all she could do was plead with them not to abandon her. She was miles away from home, her sister was dead and it would be a while before she left hospital. After talking with her for a while and reassuring her that she was going to make it out all right, the police then drove them over to Hull Kingston to formally identify their mother Joan. This they did, before sombrely heading home.

* * * *

On Sunday night, PC Bill Sullivan was back at the site on

guard duty. He had to walk back to the scene up and down the track and recover bits and pieces of bodies and various pieces of personal property of the people on board. Working with another PC, they would continue bagging up the evidence and items, recording it down and sending it to the inquiry teams. There was a lot of personal items such as handbags, all of which were catalogued in order that relatives and survivors could claim them back when they had the chance.

Once he had left the scene of the crash he would never again go there. What he saw that day has stayed with him and haunted him ever since. He has never come to terms with the scenes that greeted him and there are many aspects of the disaster that he will never talk about to anyone. Although he would speak to various relatives and survivors, even attending some of the funerals, his life would never be the same again. This was nothing like what he had seen in the past. This was no riot, no good vs. bad fight, this was definitely no street fight, no adreneline rushing battle in riot gear side by side with your police team. This was horror. Horror on a grand scale and one of which he would never forget. He would later retire from the police in 1992 due to ill health.

Chapter 5

Left to grieve

Almost as soon as the crash was in the newspapers, it was out again. By Tuesday 29th July, there was not even a mention in the daily papers, maybe the slightest bit to say that the line was now open again and the hundred yards of damaged track had been re-laid, but other than that, nothing. The disaster was already history and already forgotten by the general public. But for Richard Myerscough. Surviving the train crash was just the beginning of a long and winding road that led to seeing many people and, if possible, getting on their backs. First of all, an official contacted him and said that they've heard all about him and asked if he would do the press conference. This he agreed and was taken into a room full of photographers and journalists. All he could remember was a lot of flashing lights and flickering over the next few minutes as he described the "chaos and carnage."

Later on, when the deputy head from his school gave him a newspaper, it described him as having given the interview from his hospital bed!

MP John Prescott also rang Richard at his home and spoke to him for quite a while. He had taken an interest in this because he was a Hull MP and wanted to know what was happening with the aftermath of the tragedy. After speaking with Richard, he then went back to Parliament to ask the question of why this has now become a forgotten disaster and why are we not doing enough for the people involved?

It was not too long after the crash that he also got yet another phone call, this time from the hospital asking if he had lost his credit cards and jacket. He said that he had and it was last seen at the crash site. They said to him that it had been located and incinerated due to the blood that was stained on it. (Richard would later be able to claim this on his insurance anyway.)

With a personal interest, he began getting involved in several things relating to survivors, trauma and other disasters and went to several conferences including one in West Yorkshire, and one of the questions was "Who was responsible?" for disasters in general. This meeting was about post traumatic stress disorder.

The Royal College of Nursing in London held a conference called "When the press have gone away," and again he got invited as a speaker, with Princess Anne attending in the Royal Festival Hall of London. Psychiatrists spoke about looking at PTSD and then a vicar stood up and, according to witnesses, had a very poor attitude with him saying that basically life goes on, before telling his story about a London train crash. It would always anger Richard in the fact that if a train crashed in London it would be not be forgotten about for year, but if it was on a village level crossing in Yorkshire, you wouldn't hear of it ever again. "We didn't kill enough people" was Richard's sarcastic reply to several people over the years.

The one way that he could deal with the trauma of the crash was to make sure it didn't affect his life, so he was back on a train within a week. As soon as he got on the DMU, the first thing he noticed was the smell, and the slightest noise made him tense up. Those type of trains were very noisy at the best of times but at least he was making fast progress.

However, he still had counselling for post traumatic stress disorder and in the late 1990s he was diagnosed with ME. His counsellor said that there was nothing he could do for him as he had dealt with it very well and had done everything himself. He had started out as a school teacher in 1968, eventually retiring from the job in 2006.

* * * *

In a bizarre twist to the Ashley families' problems,

Malcolm's elder brother Aubrey was involved in an incident involving a cyclist. Travelling through Holme-upon-Spalding Moor in his lorry, he was horrified to find a nine-year-old bike rider fall in front of him and he could not avoid running over his arm. The boy was taken to hospital, where he made a full recovery; he was lucky he wasn't killed. To have two accidents in the family in just a few days was simply nothing more than a bit of bad luck.

* * * *

John Riley was a chaplain for the Railway Mission and was attending the Jubilee Conference in York when one of his colleagues came running in to him. He was between sessions and was shocked to hear his news. "John have you heard there has been a train crash – and it looks serious – at Lockington?"

This he hadn't actually heard, nor did he even know where Lockington was. Spending most of his life in York he had to look for the crash site on a map. At this moment he realised that a chaplain was the last thing that was needed there, there would be emergency crews doing important jobs and he didn't want to get under their feet or become a hindrance to them.

He held off for a while and when the time was right he contacted a very helpful sergeant at British Transport Police who put him in touch with some addresses of the families in order for him to provide support and care where it was required. He also got hold of a little medical detail too in order for him to have a better idea of what he was faced with (i.e. injuries, whether they were deceased or grieving for the deceased etc.).

So boarding a train with his pedal bike, he arrived at Driffield where his first stop was to a local estate agent where they kindly provided him with a map of the streets in the area for him to begin his work. One of the first people he went to visit, immediately assumed he was press, which is one trick that paparazzi have played in the past in order to get close to the families. However, when he assured people that he was genuine, he was welcomed into people's homes. He would go on to see most of the Driffield families and survivors, including Jason Schofield's mother (never managing to time it right to catch Jason himself though for quite a while) and the Carters.

John would continue to visit these families for many years to come and would play a very supportive role in the months and even years after the crash.

* * * *

Phil Clare had started off as a junior probation officer working out of Driffield for the Humberside Probation Service when he was first in contact with people showing signs of post traumatic stress. He was normally on his own with the senior officer out doing other tasks.

It was not long after Lockington that a survivor had become a young offender (he will remain anonymous in this book). The young lad didn't fit into the usual category of broken homes or any kind of abuse. After working with him for quite a while he gathered a lot of information on the effects major trauma has on a human, to which he teamed up with others who had been in contact with survivors of the Bradford fire of 1985 and later the *Herald of Free Enterprise*.

Social worker Michael Stewart had worked with the Bradford fire victims and Phil rang him up to arrange a meeting face to face. He told him of his work with the Lockington survivor and the problems that person had suffered with. Michael turned to him: "Is it beginning to affect your sleep?" he asked. Phil just looked and replied: "Well, yes. It is really."

Strange as it sounds, that was a good thing. He was putting himself in the position of the survivor and imagining scenes that disturbed him when he thought about them. He was finally understanding this newly discovered disorder. Together with various others, these people were now starting to be experts on what was now known as PTSD, or post traumatic stress disorder. It soon became clear that this had affected survivors of major disasters for years but never really thought about as anything worth worrying over. Physical injuries seemed more important, mental injuries should simply go away given time. But looking back over the last hundred years, it is shocking that so many signs were there right from the beginning.

* * * *

In 1988, someone invited Phil to talk in Stephen Myerscough's school about his job and the service he provided, and in the audience were Richard and Stephen. Phil said he was interested in what caused people to offend and mentioned Lockington and the work he had already been involved in. His interest was cause and effect rather than sentence. Unknown to himself there were Lockington survivors in that very room and sitting close by. Stephen went pale, so Richard made sure that he was removed from the room in a hurry. Afterwards Richard approached Mr Clare and told him that he was there at Lockington with his family and said that nobody had been there to help anyone in the months after. No part of the system seemed to have provided any help for the people suffering from trauma. After a lengthy chat, Phil agreed to a meeting in Driffield of himself and any survivors who wanted to attend. Contacting the press and the radio, a few people would turn up but not that many. Mary Foster, Hilary Harbron and the Carters were there, but in the meetings that followed, word was spread, the newspapers picked up on it and more people got involved, some starting to talk about their experiences, others remaining silent for the time being. Hilary would later say to the author: "Most people think that perhaps you don't wish to talk about it. In actual fact you want to talk about it until you drive people crazy. That was why the support group was so helpful."

Although they never kept the minutes, the Lockington Support Group was born. They met at the Bell Hotel in Driffield on a regular basis, even having a group meal at one point. Their aim was to start doing little things, such as talking about it to other victims who knew what they were going through and getting people back on trains – there were several people who would be taken on a train for the first time since the crash, just from one station to another, maybe Bridlington to Driffield, before someone would pick them up at the other end, which seemed to help a fair few people. Nobody here set up any official counselling specifically, it was left up to the individual to sort that out with their own doctors. This was basically just a group of people rallying round each other and looking after one another as they all had a connection. And it was working too!

Issues were also raised about the fact that once a disaster had hit the headlines, it was virtually forgotten about. If it was big enough and "had killed enough people" then it would stay in the memory of Joe Public. Everyone knows where they were when they heard about the September 11th attacks, Lockerbie, Princess Diana's death. But it seemed that disasters happened on an all too regular basis with a few days press coverage and then . . . nothing. No memorial. No counselling. No mention of it on the news on the fifth anniversary. The tenth. Twentieth. (I personally spoke to people living just a few miles away from the disaster who didn't even realise that there had been a major train crash just up the road.)

* * * *

Over the months and years that passed, there were occasions that were successful in getting people more aware of trauma, with Phil and Richard organising a whole training day for Social Services on PTSD. They were several speakers and a lot of people learned new things that were only just coming to light. Another conference required them to go to Skipton. At the same time John Riley from The Railway Mission got involved and attended their meetings to see how people were coping and offered help and support for those finding it too distressing.

Even the BBC got involved, making the "Open Space" series. It all started when it was advertised that they wanted people to send in suggestions on what to do the programmes on and a woman who's mother died in the IRA bombing at Enniskillen in 1987, Aileen Quinton, wrote in and gave the suggestion to do a half-hour slot on the after effects of major disasters. There had been an advert on the BBC on wanting to do this programme and

David Carter saw this. He immediately contacted them and then told Richard. It wasn't long before the camera crews arrived and came into the Myerscough's to do some interviews with Richard, Marion and Stephen, and film David Carter and the support group at the Bell Hotel in Driffield. When the programme was finished and ready, they had interviewed people involved in the *Marchioness*, Enniskillen, *Piper Alpha*, the Kings Cross fire and at Lockington. The episode was aired on BBC2 on 10th December 1990 titled "Disaster Never Ends."

Phil Clare once had to attend a conference which was trying to decide how big something had to be to be classed as a "disaster." The official result was an incident which left at least ten people killed. However, as history has shown, this is definitely not the case. Phil would later do various other work for communities affected by disasters including Hungerford after the 1987 gun massacre and Lockerbie after the 1988 aircraft bombing. (He found out that an old couple who had lived in the area of that crash had scaled a two-meter high wall in the rush to escape the burning wreckage raining down on their house, and one of these had had a hip replacement!)

Richard found that for years after the crash, smelling diesel brought back the memories of that day, although trains hold no fear for him now. The only thing is that neither David nor Richard can watch things on TV with train crashes in.

Today post traumatic stress disorder is a regularly recognised condition. In the First World War that same condition was nicknamed "shell shock" after soldiers on the front line would go into panic after constant bombings and explosions. Back in 1915 though, if you couldn't hack it and you ran away, you got shot for cowardice. Today those men have been pardoned and their reputations restored after a lengthy campaign. Over the years more and more disasters have left people in a bad state of mental affairs, as well as the wars that have been fought. You only have to read books on survivors of the two world wars, the Falklands, Iraq, and Afghanistan to know that people *need* to be looked after once their tour of duty is done. People cannot just be thrown onto the heap and classed as "services no longer required."

Today we live in an age where counselling is offered straight away. It takes a long time to recover from mental injuries like PTSD, and the sooner it is dealt with the quicker that person can make a full recovery. If not treated it can lead to depression, anxiety, break up of marriages and even suicide. This proves that PTSD is as serious as rescuing someone who has extensive bleeding trapped in the carriages of Lockington. The newspapers listed around 40 people as injured that day. There were many more than that, you just couldn't tell.

* * * *

A few members of the Lockington group joined the London-based support group "Disaster Action," which had been started by a man named Maurice de Rohan whose daughter and son-in-law died on the *Herald of Free Enterprise* in 1987. He had seen the common connections between the disasters from the mid to late 1980's and onwards and invited people to meet together to form the organisation. He got someone in the House of Lords involved too which was even better, but the problem for the Lockington survivors was that any meetings were held in London and no-one this far up country would be able to attend. After sixteen years the campaigning finally paid off with the passing of the Corporate Manslaughter and Corporate Homicide Act 2007 as well as quantum leaps in disaster management and response, which included the identifying and meeting the needs of those directly affected being central to planning and response.

However, there was much more work to be done, and Richard started on his own the Student Support Working Group held at Dove House Hospice in Hull. About half a dozen people began looking at trauma in children who had survived traumatic events like disasters and then had to return to school. The big question was . . . how was that school going to deal with this? They reported their findings and results directly back to the education authorities.

Another group was the Humberside Emergency

Response Team, which was set up not as a result of Lockington, but the support group did have a hand in it. Today they have pre-prepared plans in case such disasters happen again. They also run counselling services and go in at the early stages so the people involved can get the help required at the fastest opportunity.

* * * *

On 23rd November 1987 Stephen Myerscough was presented with a medal and certificate of meritorious conduct by the Scouts at Bridlington Town Hall for his actions at the crash site that day. British Rail then presented his Scout group with brand new camping equipment in his honour, and on top of that he had a trophy named after him – the Stephen Myerscough Trophy for First Aid – which is presented to Scouts who excel in that area. Barry Lilley of Humberside Police would later say that he "witnessed some appalling injuries for a boy of his age but nevertheless assisted injured passengers whilst he made his way along the train. He not only rendered aid to passengers but he also assisted others in their escape from the train. Stephen himself was eventually treated for bruising to his elbow and for shock."

* * * *

As far as the Wilson family would be, life had to go on.

Trevor and Maureen had to sort out his mother's belongings. It was when they first entered Joan Wilson's home again that it hit them most. On the draining board were two cups, upside down, where Joan and Lorna had shared a drink and a chat before heading towards the train station on that fateful day. It was painful enough having to go through her things, but one thing they found was interesting. There was a lot of paperwork relating to her time as a guest house landlady. One piece had words saying "Three cooked meals a day 12 and 6" (62.5p today). Her house was later sold.

Lorna would eventually leave hospital, the funeral of her sister being delayed until she was well enough to attend. None of the family would attend the inquest or the inquiry.

* * * *

Although the papers had put it down that she was a nurse, Elva O'Brien was in fact a care worker, also misspelling her daughters name as Ella instead of Helen. She went back to work not long after, thinking she was OK. She worked regular night shifts and was with a young woman who was talking to her, although she couldn't really talk back to her all night. It didn't take long for her to question what was up and she said that she understood. Elva had delayed shock and went to see the doctor who signed her off work for a while. At the end of it all she had to simply get on with life and try carry on as normal best she could.

Railway officials spoke to her and asked her if she had heard the train blow its whistle shortly before the crash, to which she replied that she did. This, they said, was vital information. They also paid for Jamie to have a ride in the fast Intercity 125 trains and sat with him on a journey from Doncaster to Chesterfield.

Since her escape from Lockington she has been struggling to erase the bad memories over the years, but unfortunately all it takes is to watch another crash on the news before it sets it all back off again. Today she still doesn't believe that Malcolm Ashley went onto the crossing on purpose and, like most people involved, bears him no ill feeling.

She would suffer more heartache when her daughter Maureen Sugden died in 1997 of lupus and over the years she has lost touch with many more of her family. As for going on trains – she has not stepped foot on one since the day of the crash.

* * * *

The Thorpe family went to Hull Royal Infirmary and were later discharged with only slight injuries. British Rail gave them a choice of how to get back to Leicester – by train or by taxi. They chose taxi. Two cars took them and another lady from that area of England back home.

BR would later give first class tickets to the family as a goodwill gesture, which they later went on holiday with. Although they received no counselling, Gordon still goes on trains today. He has since been involved in another accident, this time involving a collision with a car.

* * * *

For train guard Peter Sturdy, life would go on as normal. After the police interviewed him the day after the crash, as they did everybody who was on the train, he was told to get himself checked out. This he did and the doctor gave him a week off work before returning back to the trains. Peter was not a man to talk about things like this and he carried on with his job. However, his actions that day were not to go unnoticed. On 16th September 1986, he attended a ceremony where he was awarded a certificate of meritorious conduct by British Rail. His wife June was very proud of him and kept this framed on their wall. Up until this time, his family knew that he had attempted to stop the oncoming train but had no idea that he had gone back on board to help others. Peter would later retire from his beloved trains, spending his free time now playing golf at Sutton. He was a joker and made light of everything; he loved to make people laugh and was said to be the life and soul of any get-together. Although he would never blow his own trumpet about his actions that day, today we know he is one of the heroes of Lockington, always just acting as though he had done nothing more than just his job. In the early hours of 27th May 2001, Peter suffered a heart attack and died soon after at Hull Royal Infirmary. His wife kept his certificate on the wall and there it remains to this day. His whole family are extremely proud of him and his legacy will never be forgotten.

* * * *

Hilary Harbron walked away from the crash thinking that she was uninjured, but about three days later she realised that her left ankle was in extreme pain. She had already sprained that ankle several years ago and now the pain had returned with the trauma and violence of the crash. At this moment she also noticed that she was having problems with her neck. She was then advised to see a doctor and then a solicitor.

The neck problem got worse in a very short space of time. She would take seven weeks off work and had to have physiotherapy, being instructed to spend a lot of time lying flat on the floor.

But the biggest problem for her now was that she was afraid to go out. The only place she felt safe was in the comfort of her own home. She decided early on that she must make herself go out every other day. She never went far, maybe into Bridlington town centre and in one incident she got confused and couldn't find where she had left the car. It took half an hour of wandering around before she found it again.

Because of her injuries, she had to take early retirement from the council. She found it very hard to stay sitting at a computer all day long, and although she did continue to work longer than expected, the early retirement came as a great relief.

Today she still cannot go all day without having a 30-minute lie down on the floor. Writing is a problem for her and apart from signing cheques, everything else is typed and she sees an osteopath every six weeks. Hilary would later move to London, but even today she still keeps in touch with Mary Foster, and they regularly phone each other up. It seems ironic that such a lasting friendship could come out of something so tragic that took other friends away from each other for ever.

* * * *

For Ian Simpson, the crash didn't really affect him. The only thing that reminds him of that day is anything to do with confined spaces, including when he saw the Hillsborough football stadium disaster on TV just three years after Lockington. The little boy who he saved from being crushed and losing his legs later saw him in Driffield on main street years later and said thank you for rescuing him. He didn't recognise him at first as he was a lot older. He never had nightmares or trauma, but he did have issues with his shoulder due to the train door jolting while he was holding it for the boy's legs. Looking back, the injury was worth saving the legs of the young boy.

He didn't seek any compensation, he was just glad to be alive and well. Since that day his life has been good, he is in the IT industry, working at ReThink recruitment which he co-founded in 2005. Today he lives in North Cave with his wife and baby.

* * * *

Fireman Barry Skelton was not offered counselling, with a lot of the lads working there being told what to expect and for everyone to do their duty to the best of their ability and as best as they could. None of them needed to talk to anyone about it. Although he never got affected by it, he did think about it a lot for some time after. When he returned back to Driffield a lot of people were asking questions and he just said: "Sorry, I can't divulge any information," because a lot of people from Driffield were on board. He would attend neither the inquiry or the inquest.

The same was true also with ambulance man Bob Brown. There was no counselling for him either. Any burdens had to be discussed with other people in the same job as you as they had more or less done the same thing and would understand it more.

PC Dale Turrell realises today that he had suffered

after the crash, his family noticing a change in him over time, but since then in his job as a police officer, he has visited many scenes of death and disaster with him having various roles in the traffic sections over the two decades since. He knows now that he was deeply affected by it all but carried on as normal as he thought it was all part of the job. He did attend a meeting with other emergency services who attended at Lockington which was held about six months after the disaster in the Bell Hotel in Driffield. The main topic was identifying what PTSD was. Even today he still thinks about the crash whenever he has to cross the line where the disaster happened. As a police officer it was traumatic, as a man who lost his cousin it was double the pain.

As if the crash and the aftermath wasn't bad enough, a female hoaxer came into the picture and wrote a statement for the investigating officers for 45 minutes. She had all the parts of the story the wrong way round saying things like: "I saw the van and thought...oohh it's going to crash!" However, according to her account, the van seemed to be going in the wrong direction. After four hours, police officers were unsure if she was a credible witness who was just confused or a time waster, so they took her to the scene of the crash so she could show them what she remembered. As they approached the crossing, she tried to jump out of the police car while it was moving, and it was only the speedy reactions of one of the officers in the back that stopped her from falling out. It later turned out that she had lied on purpose to "impress" people who knew her.

* * * *

Unfortunately nowadays we live in a world where jokes are made of the worst possible things and the worst possible times. After the hoaxer came some camcorder classics. David Carter was to see something on television in very bad taste on Sunday 25th September 1994. Sitting down in front of the TV for the night, David and Jenny had the show *You've Been Framed* on. Hosted by Jeremy Beadle, the show is full of home video clips of random funnies caught on camera. People falling from trees, dogs running into their owner's groin and the things babies do without even realising it! But tonight was no laughing matter, as one of the clips showed a car at a level crossing being missed by a train with only a fraction of an inch to spare. This horrified them both and they immediately drafted a letter to Granada Television. Their argument was that, apart from bringing back terrible memories, it was nothing to laugh about and they were trying to educated drivers *not* to run red lights, not show them it pays you to not only run the crossing but to film it as well. They were immediately sent a very apologetic letter but assured them that it was a genuinely filmed by a railway enthusiast and not set up. The person who sent the film in was denied his £250 that is paid out for every clip that is shown.

* * * *

Following the crash, a police spokesman said on the radio that all their officers had been given counselling. In reality, they turned up for work as normal the day after. Keith never received any of this counselling, and neither did WPC Dyson nor the traffic policeman. The following day Dyson was sent to yet another accident scene.

Keith went on his daily life and it was about a week later that a further incident shocked him. As he approached the level crossing at Cottingham, a motorbike ran the barriers at the same time as a train was coming. Being a police officer and still with the images of the smashed train in his mind, he took down the registration number and prosecuted him.

Those images have never left him to this day, especially when he approaches level crossings. At one point he put in a request to have WPC Dyson commended for her actions that day, but it was refused, saying she had only done what everybody else had done that day, although she would later get a special mention at the inquest.

* * * *

Chaz Walker was back at work the following day after

the disaster, the line open and trains running between Bridlington to Hutton Cranswick and Beverley to Hull until the track was repaired and the line cleared at the crash site. A day or two later he decided to go to the crash site and have a look to see himself what had happened. Although he had seen the images of the news, it was more shocking than he had ever imagined. Just going to work that Saturday morning, this event had now suddenly become a major part of his life.

* * * *

Pam White rang up the hospital on Sunday morning and by then they said he was free to leave, but it was that morning that he was ready to be told by doctors that Wayne had been killed. Both Wayne and Darren had been thrown out of the window in the impact but because he had been knocked unconscious first, Darren had survived. What annoyed him the most was when a doctor saw him at home later in the day. It was a case of "Sorry you've lost your mate, life goes on, get over it," or at least it seemed that way. From that day on there were no officials or social workers who would be in touch to see how he was coping. He remained quiet about the whole affair and never spoke about it. This silence remains so to this day.

The Carters would delay moving house to Norton but only by a few days. With the funeral of Wayne taking place, the eventual house move was nothing but a blur in their days; they don't even remember doing it. Wayne's siblings would be later diagnosed with depression, while David Carter would suffer from post traumatic stress disorder. Because it wasn't actually him involved in the crash, his condition would not be recognised and he would receive no help or compensation.

Wayne was cremated at Scarborough's Woodlands Crematorium on Monday 4th August, his ashes buried at Ormesby Church in Middlesbrough, where a lot of his family were. Several generous people gave £238.35 in donations at the funeral, which was then passed on to the East Riding Voluntary Accident and Emergency Service treasurer.

After all the grief and loss, they received £3500 compensation plus legal costs, which was statutory minimum. It took three heartbreaking years to get that. British Rail considered it was not responsible for the crash and did not accept liability. However, they did reach an agreement with the National Farmers Union who insured Ashley's van, and agreed to pay 50% each regardless of who is found liable.

In a final insult, a letter arrived at the Carters in the new year of 1994 saying that they had no record of Wayne paying his national insurance contribution for the period April 1991 to April 1992 and that he is advised to pay £262.60, oh and could he pay before April or it could cost more . . . "There are time limits for paying!" After a strongly worded letter back to them, the sending out of a lette, with completely random years on anyway, was soon replaced with a letter of apology.

* * * *

The funeral of Wayne Harman took place on Monday 4th August. He was buried at Hull's Eastern Cemetery, with various members of the Lockington community turning up to pay their respects, including his head teacher.

Greg Addison's funeral was held at Driffield Methodist Church on the same day, his coffin then taken to Chanterlands Crematorium in Hull. His ashes were scattered on Emmotland Ponds near the village of North Frodingham where he used to go fishing a lot. Instead of flowers, his parents asked for donations to the Kings Mill Special School minibus appeal in Driffield.

Annette Stork was buried in Driffield Cemetery on Friday 1st August, the service taking place at Driffield Methodist Church. Because she was a very popular young woman, she got an amazing number of flowers and tributes.

Helen Lodge's funeral took place in Wetwang Parish Church, which was filled to capacity with close friends and family. She was then cremated at Scarborough, her ashes scattered in the grounds, a simple note in the book of remembrance to mark her life.

* * * *

Since 1986 then, there has only been one memorial service and that was organised by the relatives and survivors themselves on 30th July 1989. It was held in Lockington Parish Church and around 70 people attended. In a bizarre ordeal, as around 30 of them left the church and went to visit the crash site, the bad weather had affected the barriers. They were jammed down with the lights flashing and had been since 0930 that morning. A police officer in the congregation used the emergency phone to call the signal box for permission to cross so the procession could continue and for the families to lay wreathes. Ten minutes later, the BR engineers turned up to fix the fault.

* * * *

British Rail dispatched a safety adviser to the Lockington crossing not long after the disaster and after just a month they withdrew him in a barrage of protests from the locals. He had helped road users who were uneasy about crossing the line, and the villagers wanted his presence continued until the outcome of the inquiry. But this was not to be. It would take a further protest to have some kind of fail safe put there to stop this happening again. After all, it was only seven months since everything was taken away that the crash had happened. Something had to be done.

Chapter 6

Questions and lies

Once the wreckage of the train was recovered, the damaged carriages were taken away by lorry to the Dairycotes Motive Power Depot at St Andrews Dock in Hull. This huge building was owned by British Rail and would give inspectors like Neville Atkinson a chance to survey the damage and decide on what claims there were to be made. Neville worked from Doncaster Plant Works as an Estimating Technician and had been in this job for 40 years, only having another two years to go until he would eventually retire. Looking up at the monstrosities, he spent a full day going round carriages one and two, still standing on the trucks that had taken them in. It was only a few days after the crash so the events of that day were still fresh in the memory of everyone associated with the tasks, but once he had finished his inspections, he would then spend the next two to three weeks dealing with the paperwork that went with it.

Within 24 hours of the disaster, the police were round to interview the Myerscoughs, asking questions about whether they could hear the crossing sirens, was there anything wrong with the train, where he was sitting, etc. He did tell them that he was sitting above the bogeys and that they were making a funny mechanical sounding noise but that was long before being derailed and it turned out that it was normal noise for a DMU anyway. Peter Sturdy got a visit in the early evening of the 27th to write a witness statement. Two months later he received a letter to say he had to attend the inquiry as a witness: being the guard he was very important to the investigation.

Police had interviewed Malcolm Ashley and, gathering the evidence together, began preparing for a possible criminal trial, as if need be they could charge him with causing death by dangerous driving. His memory loss was very severe, not knowing anything for up to two days before the crash.

Neither he nor train driver Harry Brown would be called to give evidence at the inquiry. Originally planned for 2nd September 1986, it was decided to delay the inquiry due to several circumstances and the gathering of all the correct information, and in mid-September that year it was announced that it would take place at 10am on 7th October and following on to the 8th October 1986.

The inquiry began under the leadership of Major

Anthony King in Beverley at the Memorial Hall. King had served in the army for 23 years in the Royal Engineers and the Royal Corps of Transport, becoming a civil servant and inspecting officer for the railway inspectorate in 1973 chairing public inquiries into train accidents.

Geoffrey Isles, a lorry driver who was passing at the time of the crash and stopped, and postman Brian Mellonby were called up as witnesses who testified that the lights were working fine when the crash happened. An official representing British Rail from Hull said he turned the engines off as soon as he got there, angering Richard Myerscough. He turned to the barrister and said: "What you have just heard is a lie, I turned the engines off," but they would not call him up as a witness. (Major King wrote to him afterwards to thank him for his work that day and recognised him as being the one who switched the engines off).

It was later found out that the engines were normally protected by fuses which are there to cut the engines off in an emergency, but these fuses were gone and replaced by six inch nails! Fuses were constantly blowing on the DMU's and they were just sticking nails in to sort the problem out, but this was the reason why the engines didn't turn themselves off when the crash happened.

Major King then heard how PC Barry Cundill retraced Ashley's route from outside his home to the eventual collision spot on the level crossing and found that for a period he would have been blind to the lights due to the way they are positioned and the angle at which he drove.

Chaz Walker had to attend the inquiry and give evidence of his version of events. The signalman from Beverley went with him for one day's evidence at the inquiry. He was questioned why he did things and how he did things to make sure that they had the full picture and not missing anything vital out. As Chaz would say over two decades later: "It was very thorough questioning."

On day two of the inquiry it was revealed by BR that a signalman had seen 92 drivers ignore the red lights at a crossing near Hull, but refused to say which crossing. All they revealed was that the count was done in an eight-hour period from a signal box which had barriers. This shocked many people who never realised so many people would risk their lives just for simply saving literally a few minutes of time. Then British Rail worker Dennis Wright told the inquiry that on 13th May 1986 he saw a train go over the Lockington crossing but the lights were not working. He said that he had parked up and as he sat there he heard a train whistle and looked up to see a car going over the crossing. He got out of his cab, went over to the crossing and confirmed that there were no lights nor sirens. He checked with the signalman at Beverley who said that there was no malfunction recorded. Shortly afterwards a second train went across and the crossing equipment worked fine. Next they heard the same kind of faults from motorist Derek Leach, who claimed that the lights were faulty just three days before the disaster. He said that there were only about eight to 15 seconds of warning lights before the train passed.

After two full days of evidence from 26 witnesses, the inquiry was complete. Harry Brown was still in hospital at this time but Major King did go and see him and speak to him. It was now left up to the findings of Major King as to the cause of the disaster. It would be almost a year before that report was published.

* * * *

The inquest on the nine victims of the Lockington crash opened on 29th July at Hull and adjourned. It was led by Humberside coroner Trevor Green. It would officially continue over 24th and 25th February 1987 at the same place as Major King had held his inquiry – Beverley's Memorial Hall.

Like the inquiry, the first witnesses were called and a doctor from Hull Royal Infirmary took the stand and went through every person, giving a medical report on all who had died at the scene or as a result of the accident. All this was recorded by the coroner. The 11 people on the jury were then shown official police footage from inside the first carriage and looking out of the driver's window, then hearing the evidence of the identification of the victims, some of which had to be by the jewellery or clothing that they were wearing.

Among those who attended were the Carters, who kept out of the way of TV and newspaper reporters by going for coffee upstairs, and Chaz Walker who again had to tell them what he had done that day and that he had let the train go from Hutton Cranswick correctly and with no problems.

Carol Dyson was questioned on the crossing lights and whether they had been working or not before moving on to other matters relating to her time at the crash site. It was also revealed that if a train was travelling at normal speed heading from Bridlington, it would not have time to stop should there be an obstruction at the Lockington crossing.

But it was the evidence of Malcolm Ashley's wife Margaret that would be front page news for the local papers. She admitted to seeing the crossings lights at Lockington fail twice in one day but failed to report it to the police and this was just 16 days before her husband's crash. The first train had no warning lights or sirens, the second coming in the opposite direction later had a siren but no lights.

The following day heard evidence from the head of the police investigation, Barry Lilley, who said that there had been no less than 17 reports of malfunctions at level crossings and that some of these could not be investigated as BR had failed to log them correctly.

So after two days and 36 witnesses giving evidence, the jury decided that neither British Rail nor van driver Malcolm Ashley were to blame for the crash and returned nine verdicts of death by misadventure. In the opinion of Mr Green, the crash would not have happened if barriers had been there as there were in December of 1985. He ended the inquest by paying tribute to the bravery of Richard and Stephen Myerscough, Bill Shaw, Ian Simpson, Len Robinson and PC Carol Ann Dyson.

* * * *

On 15th September 1987 the long-awaited official report into the disaster was published and placed the full blame on Malcolm Ashley and that he had driven his van through a red light into the path of the oncoming train. It says he ignored the warning lights, which were working at the time, or may have just been distracted and failed to check the warnings. However, the resulting collision turned it from what should have been a simple derailment – i.e. just being brought off the tracks – into a major disaster. If the van had been two seconds earlier or a few inches further away then disaster would have been averted.

However Major King ruled out the theory that Ashley had deliberately run the lights in an attempt to beat the train, although he did not interview him and even if he did he had no memory of the crash anyway. Before the crash he had once remarked that anyone who tried to cross when the lights were at red "wanted their brains tested."

Because of this, Malcolm Ashley now faced a massive compensation claim including a £500,000 claim from British Rail for damage to the four carriages. However, it was decided by Humberside Police not to prosecute him and no criminal action would be taken against him. The detailed police file by this time was now in the hands of the coroner.

The report also went on to recommend an improved publicity campaign and that barriers are the safest measure to prevent another crossing crash. While 70% of open crossings are acceptable, Major King also called on the other 30% to be made safer with barriers or reduced train speeds. One of that 30% was the Lockington crossing.

Chapter 7

Legacy

Just two days after the crash, British Rail announced that it would be suspending all work on the installation of unmanned level crossings. The whole idea in the first place of having unmanned crossings with no barriers was basically to save up to £400,000 in costs. But that is no good when it is costing people their lives.

For local villager Valerie Taylor, she found out about the crash just 20 minutes after the collision. Living in Aike, she knew the Ashley family and often saw their vehicles in and around the area, and being a large family somebody always knew them. It came as a shock when it turned out that the van driver was Malcolm, who used to drive down near her house regular as clockwork every Saturday without fail. It was on the news when she first saw the images of the disaster, the roads being blocked off so couldn't get near the site even if she wanted to. As soon as she heard that it was caused by a van straying on to the line, she got together with several of the villagers and held the first of many meetings in the village hall at Lockington to discuss what, if anything, could be done to make sure this could not happen again. This first meeting had the village hall crammed with 60 people who were demanding that action be taken by British Rail to prevent further accidents on crossings.

However, it wasn't too long before the press got to know about these meetings, made the concerns their headlines and then things started to escalate. It became apparent that over the space of several months in 1985, all the villages had had their barriers removed. The locals now getting together volunteered to be part of the new-founded committee, and wrote to parish councils, main councils, unions, MPs and got support from around the country to protest on the lack of barriers. They did get some good press coverage and a lot of support as all the villagers were terrified of train accidents when they had taken the gates away but again no-one had listened to a single word that was said. Val was now the secretary with the job of getting all the paperwork sorted and letters sent, and being a general "mouthpiece" to the press and anyone else who would listen to reason. With regular weekly meetings and larger monthly meetings with other councils, the "Along The Line Action Group" was formed. They organised protests at the crossings to demand barriers be installed again. Even Hull MP John Prescott would come up to attend one of these protests. Although he only stayed for a short while, his presence did highlight the cause of the concern. Within months the group had totalled 21 incidents where the crossing warning lights at Lockington had gone wrong, in three of these cases the lights were seen to be not working at all. All these incidents had taken place between December 1985 (when the barriers were taken away) and July 1986 when the crash happened.

Locals were now coming forward to say that they had seen several faults with the crossing before the crash. People say they saw a train go across with no lights flashing, no siren, or sometimes there was siren and lights but no train. On 5th September, just 41 days after the crash, a driver reported a near disaster at the very crossing. He was just three feet away from the Lockington crossing when the amber light flashed once. By the time the red light was flashing the train was already going across in front of him, with not warning siren either. If it wasn't for him braking suddenly, the tragedy could have been repeated so very soon. BR just said of the incident that "it didn't make sense." These incident reports piled up and before long the group had clearly something to go on. Countless collisions on the local crossings and various faults gave the campaign strength and the press soon picked up on it. The group announced that they had six main aims:

1) Higher safety standards at all crossings;

2) Full barriers with TV monitoring and fail safe back up at all automatic crossings;

3) A man to be retained at the existing stations;

4) Radio contact to be maintained between train drivers and signalmen;

5) A man to be placed at all open crossings to monitor trains and equipment;

6) Seek support from all appropriate bodies to achieve these aims.

The biggest obvious one was to get full barriers installed – at Lockington and Cranswick especially.

One Sunday in November 1986 over 100 people turned up at the Cranswick crossing holding banners, and joining them was Bridlington MP John Townend. Other protests were joined by school friends of Wayne Harman. Holding signs like "Barriers bring express relief" and "Barriers to BR," also present were members of a South Woodham (Essex) group doing the same thing. They had started up WATCH – Woodham Against The Crossing Hazard. They met with members of Along the Line and together the two groups took part in the protest.

Before long they got a visit from 59-year-old Professor Peter Stott, who was compiling a report on behalf of the government into the country's open level crossings, and Along the Line was the only group he was taking the trouble to meet. He spoke with the campaigners, by now growing to the size of several local villages together. The group was formally invited to give its research to Prof Stott to use in his collation of information. For this, other surveys were carried out to gather more information, including sitting next to the crossing for a week between 7am till 8pm taking note of barriers, timings, lights, traffic and trains. Their research over the months found that:

1) Open crossings, especially AOCR's (Automatic Open Crossing Remotely Operated), have a very bad and increasing accident record; these risks are unacceptably high.

2) Open crossings make no allowances for human error or foolishness and none for adverse weather conditions. A physical barrier is vital to help provide a "failsafe" for the road-user.

3) Many other countries, e.g. France, Spain, Sweden and the USA, have tried automatic open crossings and are phasing them out.

4) AOCR's seem subject to malfunctioning. This fact tends to encourage road-users to adopt a disrespectful – even blasé – attitude to red flashing lights.

5) Urgent attention must be given to the introduction of radio contact between signalmen and train drivers, where automation is to be introduced. At

present, a signalman is powerless to halt a train which has already entered a very long track section, even though he may have been advised of an obstruction. This is an additional, unacceptable risk to the users of automatic open level crossings.

The Stott report into open level crossings was published in August 1987 after a research period of ten months, and as a result, 75 open crossings would get action in either reduced train speeds or half barriers. ASLEF, the train drivers' union, wrote to Prof Stott calling for all open crossings to be fitted with full lifting barriers with CCTV control at all automatic crossings in Britain.

Just over a year after the crash, thanks to the Stott report, British Rail agreed to have *half* barriers put up. This was better than nothing, as originally they had stood firm in the fact that they were not having anything there at all, so the group were delighted when these barriers were agreed. Originally these barriers were going to be installed on July 26th until they realised it was the first anniversary of the Lockington crash so the date was changed. The following month the barriers were installed and remain so to this day, a testament to the hard work and sheer determination of a group of locals who were hell bent on making sure the legacy of Lockington would be a change for the better. With a job well done, the action group was disbanded.

Today the Lockington crossing, which had caused so much trouble and heartache, has an AHB, or Automatic Half Barrier. When the train comes, the amber light shows for three seconds and goes onto the twin red flashing lights. Around four to six seconds later the barriers begin to lower and take around a further six to ten seconds more. Trains would not arrive until no less than 37 seconds have passed since the amber lights first show. The alarm will sound from the moment the amber light shows until the barriers begin being raised again. The crossing is monitored at Beverley and if there are any faults recorded, the train is immediately stopped and a crossing keeper is sent out to investigate.

* * * *

Although the Lockington crash was a tragic event in the history of the rail network, it also brought out a number of people who would shine above all others, who would put themselves last in the hope of getting a job done that would ease the pain and suffering of someone else. When all the investigations were complete, these everyday heroes would emerge one by one and in some cases were recognised by the companies and press.

British Rail would later send a letter to Brigadier Peter Marzetti thanking the 27 members of the Army School of Mechanical Transport at Leconfield for their work at the scene of the crash that day. Their help in setting up a food stall and bringing lifting equipment was second to none.

Stephen Myerscough got a meritorious medal of bravery from the Scouts for his actions that day. He was presented with this at the church in Bridlington's Chapel Street (which has since been demolished). British Rail also gave the Scouts camping equipment to use (some of which is still used today). On top of that the Scouts began the Stephen Myerscough Award for First Aid, a trophy which would be presented to different members of the Scouts who would excel in this field. At the same time as Stephen received the Scouts award, the families and survivors got a free first class rail ticket to go anywhere they wanted, although funnily enough they never did use it. As far as the crash itself affecting his life, Stephen had to have counselling to get over it. He's now married and living in Bristol.

* * * *

Jason Schofield took the crash worse than most people. He suffered from very bad depression and needed counselling. He still has problems with his neck today, although the only physical scar is on a finger. He would have recovered over time would it be for not more than one personal tragedy. Four of his friends have been killed in tragic circumstances since he watched Greg Addison die. Every time this happens he is pulled back into the past, making his depression worse. Years after the crash he was diagnosed with post traumatic stress disorder, where he would get flashbacks of being back on the train, wake up in the middle of the night after having the images of glass showering his face replayed again and again in his mind.

The Railway Mission, a support group from the train company, came round to see him for many years, offering help and advice. They would go round to many of the survivors and provided much-needed support and comfort, and were very welcome into the homes of the Carters and the Myerscoughs.

Jason did attend a session of the Lockington Support Group but it just didn't do much for him and never went back. The police interviewed him as part of their inquiry but for all his suffering he got statutory minimum compensation of around £4,000. It was getting back into snooker that made him feel like he was honouring Greg's memory. The club they played in together had a special cup made and called it the "Greg Addison Trophy" and by coincidence it was Jason who was the first to win it in 1987. He would later go on to do a 12-hour snooker marathon in his memory, raising £307.84 for the upkeep of the Kings Mill School minibus. Today Jason still sees people from the crash and would share a drink with the likes of Ian Simpson and Jordan Donnelly. But for Jason, time is not a healer. With all his friends dying over the space of 23 years, he still sees a counsellor and has regular sessions.

It was ten years after the crash that he returned to the crossing to place flowers and has returned every year, if he could make it, to pay his respects to his pal Greg and the other victims. He spoke to a woman at one of the houses who recognised him as the man who she gave a cup of tea to. Jason still goes to the crossing every July to lay flowers and will do for many years to come.

Jim Bloom would never forget running up the line to help the injured, but it would be years later that he very nearly became involved with a similar accident. It was 12th April 1996 at the Scorborough level crossing, just down the line from Lockington, that a near disaster occurred. Jim's six-year-old grand-daughter Jessica was being picked up from school by a family friend who also collected her own children. The barriers were manually operated and basically you would watch for a train coming and if the coast was clear and the lights weren't flashing you could open the barriers and go across. However, the barriers had been left open and as they drove up to the crossing the train came and smashed into the car, taking the front part clean off. The woman and three children were very shaken but otherwise unhurt. It was at this point that Jim's wife started to campaign for automatic barriers at the crossing. This was yet another example of a poorly designed level crossing. How many more misses are there going to be before another Lockington? In the end, the crossing was upgraded and made automated.

* * * *

The Stork family were hit hard by the loss of Annette. Her sister Julie was seven months pregnant at the time and the shock of her death had her in hospital until her baby Amy was born on the 19th September that year. There have been rumours since of her being pregnant but in the end that's all it was, just rumours. A padre from The Railway Mission would come round for several years, like a few of the families, and provided much needed support. From the train crash at 10am that day, it had taken until 10pm that night to have official confirmation of Annette's death, all of which was extreme worry for the whole family. But over the years times changed and the family moved on, never forgetting Annette and the 23 years of joy and happiness she had brought her parents. Later a Jewish friend of the family would plant five trees in Israel in her memory, sending Christine a certificate which today hangs on her wall. Sadly, Annette's father Melvin died in August 2008. He was buried with his daughter in Driffield cemetery.

One-year-old baby Jordan Donnelly had no real physical injuries from the crash and was cared for by his father Herbert. However, it was when he was around five years old that he started waking up in the middle of the night saying that he could hear a loud bang. This went on for quite a while and he was taken to see a child psychologist. It seemed that although Jordan had no memory of the crash, that day was mentally etched into his head and was replaying several years later. Because of the fact he was in the crash himself and that he had lost his mother, he received a considerable sum of money which was put in a trust fund by Annette's mother Christine until he was 18.

Over the years he gradually knew more about his mother, although at one point he shut down his emotions on the subject and refused to talk about it. However, Christine had saved various newspaper articles for him to read about how his mother died and the Lockington crash in general and even Herbert's father would tell him that his mother was a "very quiet girl, a nice wee girl."

At the time of writing this book, Jordan has never visited the site where his mother died; he feels it would be strange to see where the crash occurred.

* * * *

Sue Dales went back to work for Lloyds Bank. She ended up going on her holiday to Tenerife as planned, as it was said that it would do her good to get away. Because she lost consciousness straight away and woke up in hospital, she did not have any issues with post traumatic stress and thankfully missed out on seeing the most horrendous scene you could imagine. Today she still works for Lloyds TSB and is married. The only thing that identifies her connection with Lockington is the scrapbook she kept at the time and the fact that she has still got lump in top middle of her back, where today finds that she can't lean over things too long as it will ache if she does. Only Ian Simpson knows how lucky she really was at surviving the crash as he saw everything that happened to her.

* * * *

On the first anniversary of the crash, Richard Myerscough and Bill Shaw went back to the crossing and paid their respects to the people who died. At 10am the 9.33 from Bridlington rumbled past in a chilling echo of what should have happened a year previous. He was photographed by the local press standing silently at the track side, his head bowed.

* * * *

Darren White would never forget his friend Wayne Telling. The crash had left him feeling guilty that he had survived and that Wayne had died. He was heavily traumatised and the sight of a train gave him a racing heart and sweating as he was again brought back into carriage one at Lockington. The thought of going back on a train would be completely out of the question. But unlike others, Darren would never talk about it to anyone, even his closer family. The reason is that he gets too emotional about it and it is his way of dealing with it. If he blocks it out then the memories cannot hurt him. (This was only broken 24 years later when the author interviewed him for this book. Darren recalled Wayne when he spoke about him in August 2010 as "my best friend. He was loyal, dependable, always up for a laugh and I can't remember us ever falling out with each other, he was so easy going. He loved Middlesbrough FC and he would have loved it when they reached the Premier League and had some relative success. He had been at school in Northallerton so we didn't see as much of each other in the year leading up to the accident. He lost his life at a time when he had developed into a fantastic young man entering an exciting and fresh part of his life.")

As far as his life was concerned, he joined a football team with a few of the lads from Driffield School, so when he returned to class in the September of 1986 it wasn't as bad as he thought it could be. Leaving school, he worked on farms for a while, where one day he saw that the person delivering calves to the dairy farm was none other than Malcolm Ashley. At the time he was naturally angry towards him, but today he feels nothing bad and knows that Malcolm is just as much a victim as the rest of them. So, after years of doing various jobs in farming over the years, he wanted a career that would give him immense job satisfaction. He successfully applied and joined the West Yorkshire Fire Service in 2000 and has loved it ever since. The scars of Lockington are still visible on the right side of his head and his leg clicks when he moves it in a certain way. But with his job as a firefighter, it now seems ironic that the rescued has now become the rescuer.

* * * *

PC Carol Dyson would stay in Humberside Police, moving around the area over the years. Although she knew about the comments about her hat, it seemed that other people were more concerned than she was, going back to work and doing as she was told without question. Even today people tell her that their lasting memory of that day was the hat! It would be months before people would try and talk to her about the crash, to make sure it hadn't affected her, but by that point it was too late for counselling. She had already spoken to her mother the night of the disaster and some of her colleagues hadn't even had that luxury! She has never been back to Lockington crossing.

For PC Howard Brown, he too would never return to the crash site, after leaving the scene at around 5pm that day. He too is still a serving member of Humberside Police, being promoted to Sergeant in 1990. By the fourth anniversary in 1990 there were still a large number of people waiting for compensation. By this time though things were getting out of hand. British Rail were dragging things out while liability was proven, the injured were forced to accept the standard settlements as they could no longer afford to fight it. Costs went up, bills came in and the payments just didn't seem to be going their way. This angered a lot of the survivors and relatives as by now the compensation would have made considerable interest for the guilty parties in their own accounts.

A lot of the people on that train would now be classed as the forgotten victims. With post traumatic stress disorder awareness in its very early stages, not a lot was done to help those who woke up in cold sweats in the middle of the night or were too afraid to go out. Before long the disaster had been totally wiped from most people's memory, remembered only by the few who were there or the locals who had heard of it through the grapevine.

As the years rolled by it became apparent that the public sympathy and support generated after the Zeebrugge disaster would not be the same for Lockington. It was a quiet village disaster which happened on a Saturday, didn't kill a huge number of people unlike the major ones in London and anyway the line was open again a few days later. All's well that ends well then. In actual fact the anger that now rose for the local people who didn't even give the survivors a second thought now boiled to the surface. No help was offered, no sympathy was given, and worst of all they were simply forgotten.

* * * *

For Amanda West things took an unexpected turn in her life. Soon after the crash she began having nightmares, sitting bolt upright in bed and screaming, this happening for months at a time. The only people she discussed the crash with was her foster parents and social workers. She tried getting on a train to Hull again several years later but hated it. She was very nervous the whole journey, even talking randomly to two elderly women who were having their own conversation. "I had to join in with them, I had to talk to someone . . . about anything. It was the only way I would kind of forget about the train ride." This did not quell her fear of trains and today she still avoids them. If she can she avoids going across any level crossings.

She would neither seek nor claim compensation and like everyone else on the train didn't get her ticket refunded (although technically she *did* actually complete the journey to Beverley).

But the morning of the fourth anniversary of the crash changed her life forever when she gave birth to her son Ben, who was born at 9.17am, just 43 minutes away from the exact time the train crashed. From that day July 26th was a day to celebrate, not to mourn. Naturally she still thinks about the crash every year on that day, but now it is a day of happiness.

* * * *

The wrecked carriages from the crash were removed in an operation lasting just a few days. The huge crane slowly lifted them up and placed them on the side of the track to be taken away. Once all investigations were completed, carriages three and four were put back into service. As for the remains of carriages one and two, they were wrapped in a double layer of plastic sheeting and buried at Willerby landfill site just two months after the disaster. The reason for this, it is said, was that, although every precaution had been taken to remove the asbestos, there was still a risk of dust particles escaping. Being wrapped in plastic and covered with tons of earth seemed alarming to the survivors and they began to make phone calls asking what the long-term effects this may have on health and what did they do with all the other DMU's that were no longer used. In the end it turned out that there were no health implications and it had been done purely as a precautionary measure. Those carriage remain buried to this day.

* * * *

Richard Myerscough got compensation from BR for his coat but other than that he didn't make any other claim as he was not injured. However, he did make a claim for his rail ticket saying his journey had been interrupted and not made. Like Ian Simpson, the Carters and everyone else who tried to claim their fare back, he never heard back from them.

* * * *

Wayne Telling's exam results were revealed later that summer. He had passed with very good grades in English, Geography, Mathematics, Physics, Chemistry and Biology. David and Jenny Carter today look back to their time with Wayne as a happy time with fond memories, and although Wayne has been gone for over two decades, those memories will never fade away.

* * * *

Train driver Harry Brown never recovered from his injuries, always suffering from aches and pains caused by the amount of surgery. He retired from the trains after spending a total of 38 years on the job and would later pass his days at an allotment. Occasionally talking about the crash now and then, he died at his home in Bridlington in January 1990 after never getting better from the events of that fateful day.

* * * *

Hull Kingston General, where the bodies of the victims were held after the crash, closed down in 2000 after a career lasting 160 years. The main hospitals in the area today remain Hull Royal Infirmary and Castle Hill Hospital at Cottingham.

* * * *

Bill Shaw would be back in the headlines in 2001 when his wife would be a survivor of the Great Heck train crash near Selby. Ten people died when a car towing a trailer crashed through a barrier on a motorway and ended up on the railway line. As the driver was ringing for the emergency services, a train hit the wrecked car and derailed. Everyone would have been okay but then along came a goods train which was early and slammed into the derailed passenger train. The driver was later jailed for five years for falling asleep at the wheel, an accusation he has always strongly denied. Like Malcolm Ashley, this disaster will now live with him for the rest of his life.

* * * *

Lorna Wilson survived her injuries and trauma and managed to attend her sister's funeral. She lived a long life and always used to keep in touch with her family. She died in 2007 aged 89.

* * * *

Although level crossings have been made safer, road users still believe that they are invincible when it comes to racing towards the track to beat the barriers. Time after time we are shown on the news images of cars only just being missed by a high speed train, a lorry speeding through a red light to have the barriers crash down on top of the trailer and not to mention the hundreds of suicides that take place every year on the British railway network.

It was 6th November 2004 when the horrors of Lockington were tragically relived but in slightly different circumstances. A high-speed train struck a car on the track at a level crossing in Ufton Nervet, Berkshire, and subsequently derailed. In the smashing up of the train, seven people were killed and over 100 were injured. After a lengthy investigation it was confirmed that the driver of the car had purposely lain in wait on the track in order to commit suicide. Today a memorial garden marks the spot where, like Lockington, tragedy struck a normal everyday level crossing, although this one had barriers and the crash was intentional.

However, Lockington still remains a very much unique accident. Hixon and Ufton are the only two other instances where vehicles on the track have caused a train crash. Hixon in 1968 was a slow-moving road transporter crossing the track and Ufton Nervet was an intentional suicide. The 1986 Lockington crash is the only British rail crash where a car has accidentally strayed onto the railway line and then derailed the train causing multiple death and injury.

After all the hype about the spate of rail accidents in the late 1990's/early 2000's, it still remains to be noted that train travel is generally safe. That does not alter the fact that it is everybody's responsibility to ensure safety is adhered to around railways, whether at crossings, stations, underground tube systems or even on road bridges. If everyone looks out for one another then together we can all make sure that tragedies such as Lockington will never happen again. In theory.

* * * *

For the van driver, Malcolm Ashley, his life would never be the same again. He was eventually discharged from hospital on 10th August 1986 after suffering from a fractured skull and various other injuries. Because he had no memory of the crash he was unable to help with any questions regarding the collision. He had lost his foster son, become injured himself and was blamed for the worst train crash in East Yorkshire for 59 years. For the families of the dead and injured, most lay no blame at his door. A lot of them are friendly towards him and bear no grudge. He carries on his farm work to this day not far from the crossing which changed his life forever. Naturally he would want to forget about it as much as possible. To this day he stays silent on the morning that brought carnage to a small East Yorkshire village crossing.

Left: The first editions of the *Hull Daily Mail*, a local evening newspaper, carried the first images and details of the crash, although at this point the death toll was thought to be ten.

Right: The Hull Daily Mail kept the story front page on Monday 28th July with stories from the survivors and rescuers.

Left: *The People* newspaper had the correct death toll but also said that Wayne Harman was still alive.

Right: Monday's *Yorkshire Post* had three full pages of coverage including in depth stories and interviews

A photograph taken after the burial of Annette Stork showing how many flowers were placed there at Driffield Cemetery.

Annette's grave today. She is buried with her father Melvyn who died in 2008.

Christine Quinn and Elsie and Herbert Marsters were buried together in Hull. Unfortunately the name Marsters is mis-spelled.

The grave of 11-year-old Wayne Harman at Hull's Eastern Cemetery.

Beverley Memorial Hall where the inquiry and inquests were held in the months following the disaster.

Protests at local crossings.

Protests at Hutton Cranswick crossing.

Patrick Wall MP (middle) with Graham Chapman (right with glasses) of Lockington Parish Council.

Protests at Hutton Cranswick crossing.

Meetings at Lockington village hall following the disaster.

Graham Chapman and Mary Munro-Hill hold another Parish Council meeting to a packed hall.

More meetings included various "Along the Line" campaigners including Valerie Taylor (far right at the back wearing white top looking downwards).

Meetings at Lockington Village Hall

On the first anniversary of the crash, Richard Myerscough stands in remembrance at the site of where the train came to rest.

The scene at the Memorial Hall, Beverley at the start of the inquiry, 7th October 1986.

The 1989 memorial service at the crossing where the barriers were stuck down. The Stork family are among the front of the congregation.

The Bell Hotel in Driffield where the Lockington Support Group met and were also filmed for the BBC Open Space programme in 1990.

Christine Stork, mother of Annette, received this from a Jewish friend to say that five trees were planted in Israel in memory of her.

Left: Peter Sturdy's award for meritorious conduct from British Rail.

Right: Stephen Myerscough's award for meritorious conduct from the Scout Association.

Left: Stephen also had this first aid trophy made in his honour which has since been won by several Scouts.

Bridlington Free Press
announce Stephen's award on
26 November 1987.

The carriages are buried at the Willerby land fill site wrapped in plastic.

The crash site today, the crossing having automatic half barriers.

Hilary Harbron in 2004.

Annette Stork's son
Jordan Donnelly today.

The unveiling of the memorial
by Richard Myerscough (left)
and David Carter(right).

East Yorkshire MP
Graham Stuart,
David Carter, Richard
Myerscough, Richard
Jones (author) and
Driffield Mayor Paul
Rounding stand at the
memorial.

Flowers at the memorial.

Howard Brown at the memorial opening.

Left: Jason Schofield meets Mary Foster who reminds him that he gave her a mint in the hospital bed!

Carol Ann Slater (nee Dyson) meets Mary Foster for the first time since she helped rescue her.

Jason Schofield's snooker skills won him the Greg Addison trophy a year after the crash and also a snooker marathon raised over £300 for the Kings Mill School minibus. When the bus was scrapped the plaque was saved and framed with photos of the bus.

The Driffield Times, 2nd July 1987.

Snooker Cup Pictured above at the Cue Sports and Social Club, Driffield, after the Greg Addison Cup snooker competition are (left to right): Chris Flintoft, winner Jason Schofield, referee Peter Holgate, runner-up Simon Oxlade, Mrs Doreen Addison, Mr Collin Addision and Brian Walmsley.

A snooker marathon, held in memory of Lockington rail disaster victim Greg Addison, has raised £307.84 towards the upkeep of the new Kings Mill School minibus. Participants Jason Schofield and John Dowling handed over the money in a bucked to the school's headmaster Mr Peter Montgomery, at the Cue Sports and Social Club in Anderson Street, Driffield. Our picture shows, from left to right, Mr Paul Baker (marathon referee), Jason Schofield, John Dowling, Mr Montgomery, his son Eric Montgomery, and Mr Derek Walmsley (marathon referee).

The Driffield Times, 7th May 1987.

Greg Addison minibus plaque.

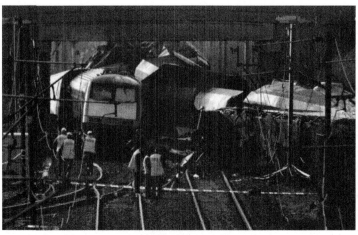

Great Heck crash, 2001.

Ufton Nervet
crash, 2004.

Epilogue

Over the years there have been many train accidents and disasters. Some have happy endings with everyone getting off alive, but others not so fortunate. It did shock me that Lockington was the 79th worst train crash in Britain. It also shocked me that such a disaster was forgotten in all but a few memories. When I began my interviews for this book in 2009, the general feeling was that a memorial was a good idea and that it had been a long time in coming. There had been a desire for one from the Lockington Support Group right from the beginning, and with a few generous donations from the time, the idea for a memorial was discussed between relatives and survivors.

Some of these designs included having nine trees planted in a memorial garden in or around Driffield School, where several victims and survivors had attended. However, it seemed that several people again objected as they did not wish to go to school every day with a constant reminder of that day in their midst.

However it soon became apparent that whatever was

discussed, it would be not satisfactory to one person, it would not be right, it would not be what they had in mind etc., so the idea for the memorial started being more hassle that it was worth. Bearing in mind these people have their own issues with PTSD and also of losing a loved one, the last thing they wanted was to get involved in a losing battle and cause yet more unnecessary heartache and stress.

So as sad as it was for many of the people involved that day, the idea of a memorial didn't go any further than a discussion and people got on with their lives, with the odd press report on the tenth anniversary questioning why there was still nothing to remember those killed.

That is, until August 2009. I began Lockington as just another project. If I got enough information to write a book then all would be good. If not it would be shelved and forgotten about while I got on with other things. But to my astonishment this was not to be. The Driffield Times ran the story first of all with my idea that there should still be a monument to the crash and with that in mind the paper printed my details and within days I had a stream of phone calls from all kinds of people involved with the disaster.

The memorial idea was one of the first questions I asked about when I eventually met up with the likes of David and Jenny Carter, Jason Schofield and Richard Myerscough (to name but a few!). At first I don't think many people believed that it would come to anything, although they still agreed to be interviewed and wished me well with my quest. They did however say that a memorial and a book was a "brilliant idea" and said it should have been done a lot sooner.

It was then I managed to get in touch with Lockington church council who ran the church and asked them for permission to place some kind of headstone type memorial in the churchyard. At first this was greeted with enthusiasm and they had a meeting to discuss this. This made me very pleased as it was obviously being taken seriously and with a bit of luck they will all grant permission. The plans were put forward to the Diocese of York (who run all the churches in East Yorkshire) and the waiting game began.

Not long after my initial proposal, the church council got back to me and said that if I wanted all the names on the stone then I would need permission from the relatives of all the nine victims. Incredibly I did manage to track them all down, but a confrontation with one particular person who cared nothing for the fact that there was not just one name but nine, meant that I could not place the names on there. Back to square one.

"OK," I said. "How about a smaller stone just literally saying In Memory of the nine who died?" was my response. Again another meeting, another month. And then another brick wall. The York Diocese would not allow any free standing stone in Lockington church yard, but would allow a plaque to go on one of the gateposts. "Although it is a very monumental gatepost" was the conversation when I rang them up. "It will even make your memorial look grander than just having a simple plaque."

Sounds good, I thought. "All you need is the relevant forms filled in and a letter from the Lockington Church Council saying that they approve." No problem. Or so I thought. The Lockington church council had already discussed this previously and under no circumstances wanted a plaque on the gate post. They would settle only for a free standing memorial. I rang the Diocese back, to which I was told they would settle only for a plaque and under no circumstances would allow anything free standing. I told them that I had been playing verbal tennis with the Diocese and council for nine months now and had got absolutely nowhere. I needed a compromise that satisfied both parties as well as the victims and families. They told me to just keep applying with different designs but when I pointed out that each design gets rejected every time the reply was simply "Not my problem." This made me furious!

When I have studied disasters in the past, I have always liked to visit the memorial and pay silent respect to those who have died and actually see where the event in question took place. I have visited Kings Cross (Fire

1987, Terrorist bomb 2005), Lockerbie (air crash 1988), Clapham (train crash 1988) to name just a few.

What struck me is that there had been several headline-hitting train crashes over the years with a fair few having a death toll of less than Lockington and they had all had some kind of tribute. Both Great Heck (2001) and Ufton Nervet (2004) had memorial gardens, Hatfield (2000) and Paddington (1999) featured in a drama documentary, Southall (1997) and again Great Heck had been the subject of documentaries interviewing the survivors and relatives. All these major incidents had been splashed across the newspapers with pages and pages of coverage, to run on for months while the investigations, inquiries and in some case trials were taking place. Other memorials were put up for the big crashes over the years but for some reason it was Lockington that took the back seat.

The campaign to have a memorial was still ongoing for me and I wouldn't have been surprised if the people who I had interviewed had had little faith in me. First of all, money needed to be raised. With £300 in an old account from the 1980s, I got the odd £10 here and there, maybe a £20 or £50 but this was coming in slowly and I wanted things to happen now. It was then the thought came of doing a sponsored walk from Bridlington to Driffield. Immediately I went round local shops in both towns asking for sponsors. Many people gave to the cause, one man giving me whatever change was left over from his lunch, which was 37p. This I began to really enjoy, because it showed that people cared and some even told me personal stories of spending time with one of those who died or remembering something from that day. (On the flip side there were some people who were rude and absolutely unreal in their attitude. I don't think they realised that if they just said "no" I would go away. Some didn't even know that the crash had occurred just a few miles up the road!)

The walk took place on 12th February 2010 and it turned out to be just me and my mother. After a long trek through grass verges and empty drinks cans we finally made it in about six hours. My wife Victoria picked us up and we were met with complimentary drinks at the Bell Hotel. A job well done even if I did say so myself (and I must admit that was the most welcomed pint I have ever had after walking for miles!)

After hitting too many brick walls with the idea of the memorial in Lockington church, I decided to focus my attention on a different location. One that would be significant yet welcome. Then it suddenly dawned on me. A small article in the Hull Daily Mail mentioned that funds were wanted to re-erect a war memorial in the North End Garden in Driffield. Now it didn't say it was Driffield WAR memorial garden, so I contacted the local town council and spoke to a very pleasant woman called

Claire who immediately put it to the next meeting. Within a week I had my answer. It had been unanimously approved to place a memorial to those killed at Lockington in Driffield Memorial Gardens. I could not believe it! It had been literally days to decide this whereas everywhere else had dithered and grumbled. It immediately went to East Riding of Yorkshire Council, who also approved and again to the Friends of North End Park who were delighted. I was ecstatic.

I immediately began organising a ceremony and to get the memorial itself made. Almost straight away it was on the front page of the Hull Daily Mail – by coincidence they were running an article that day anyway on Richard Myerscough and his story as part of a 125th anniversary of the newspaper and the people who have made the news. The money for the rest of the stone came in slightly quicker and I had the pleasure of telling many families that there was at last going to be somewhere to remember the disaster. People were calling me from all over including Jason Schofield who was more than happy. "I can't believe it's going to be right on my doorstep!" was his reaction.

So now I had to organise the ceremony itself and the best time to do it was on Sunday 25th July 2010, the day before the 24th anniversary.

* * * *

Not long after I had interviewed Bob and Mary Bayes for this book, Bob died on 28th January 2010. This I found out when I started going round everybody who I had spoken to inviting them to the ceremony. I contacted the local newspapers and the BBC who had already taken a keen interest in the project and they all said that they would turn up. I worked closely with Richard Myerscough to sort out an event that would suit everybody and at the same time give a full public thank you to those who had put their full effort in that day saving lives and limbs. As I was working on my speech the emails and phone calls were coming in at a steady pace from people wanting to know more. I had a list of 50 people who would be coming for definite so at least we knew there would be a small crowd at least.

So at 1pm on the Sunday I turned up to the memorial, which by now had been up for two days to allow it to settle. Covered in foam wrap and tape, I ripped it all off and saw for the first time the stone in all its glory. My wife and I covered it up with a green cloth which would keep it from people until the time was right. Within minutes people were turning up, Elva O'Brien had come all the way from Barnsley, the man with the PA system so everybody could be heard. The Myerscoughs had brought a couple of chairs for Mary Foster and Hilary Harbron. BBC Look North and the Hull Daily Mail came straight to me not long after to do a quick bit on camera to save time later. As the 2pm start approached there was over 120 people gathered around the memorial. The whole Stork family was there, Jason Schofield, Pam and Darren White, David and Jenny Carter, representatives of Northern Rail, Humberside Police and Humberside Fire and Rescue, all of whom were in uniform. Then there was the East Yorkshire MP Graham Stuart and the Driffield Mayor Paul Rounding. The scene looked amazing, all these people here to remember those nine lives which were cut short 24 years previously. As I began the opening speech the cameras rolled. I welcomed everybody before turning over to Richard Myerscough, who spoke about the crash itself and gave thanks to those who helped at the scene and those who were there to assist afterwards. John Riley from the Railway Mission stood up next to talk about his involvement and say a few words before calling for a minute's silence to remember the dead. I could see a few tears in the audience as Richard and David Carter got the bottom of the cloth and pulled it off the monument. The press cameras went ecstatic, as for the first time the Lockington disaster was finally remembered, set in stone. It all became too much for a few people to went to one side to compose themselves.

Again it was my turn to talk as I gave the closing speech. I personally thanked the work the emergency services do today, the people who made the memorial happen, Driffield Town Council, East Riding of Yorkshire

Council, Friends of North End Park and not forgetting JG Gardiner's of Bridlington who made the stone. I then told everybody why it had taken so long to get the memorial in place. As I wrapped up the ceremony I invited people to join the Facebook group to leave their memories, to contact me if they would like to add to this book, to join us for drinks in the Rose and Crown straight after and to lay floral tributes at the Lockington memorial. After a round of applause the relatives started coming forward with flowers and lay them at the base of the stone.

It was here that people started coming up to me and thanking me for the hard work and that there was at last somewhere to remember the dead. Carol Slater (nee Dyson) came to me and asked if the woman that she had saved all those years ago was here. I said yes she was and as I led her over, the cameras followed. I approached Mary Foster and said: "Mary, there's somebody here I want you to meet." To which Carol told her that it was her that had helped get her out of carriage one. This meeting was filmed and broadcast, a very moving moment. Not long after I got Mary and Jason Schofield together, who had not seen each other since they lay together in hospital that day. "I remember you offered me a mint," she said to him. "But I couldn't get it in my mouth," and they both laughed at the memory of a small incident on such a tragic day.

For me the work was almost over. A few more people gave me their phone numbers and said they would help me with my research, others just said thank you and how lovely it was and that it was in the right place in such beautiful settings. After shaking hands non-stop and having a general chit-chat, I had a few drinks over the road and went home. The Lockington memorial today stands proud in the North End memorial garden for all those who want to remember the disaster to have a quiet and peaceful moment with their thoughts. For the nine who died, they will now always be remembered.

Acknowledgements

This book would not have been possible without the help of a great number of people. Doing this project has introduced me to some caring, friendly and in some cases fascinating people. For all your help, I thank you for everything.

Driffield Times/Post

Bridlington Free Press

Hull Daily Mail

Yorkshire Post

Ross Parry Agency

Mirrorpix

BBC Look North

Office of Rail Regulation

ASLEF

Hull Library

Beverley Archives

Lloyds TSB

National Railway Museum

Radio Humberside

Bell Hotel, Driffield

Northern Trains

HM Coroner, Hull

Disaster Action

Driffield Town Council

East Riding of Yorkshire Council

Friends of North End Park

J G Gardiner Ltd

Leicester Mercury

Barnsley Chronicle

David and Jennifer Carter

June Sturdy

Jane Jordan

Pam White

Lorraine Beasley

Trevor and Maureen Wilson

Richard Wilson

Christine Stork

Barrie Harman

John Marsters

Richard and Marion
Myerscough

Mary Foster

Ian Simpson

Hilary Harbron

Jason Schofield

Sue Wardill

Amanda Thornton

Jordan Donnelly

Elva O'Brien

Kathleen Thorpe

Gordon Thorpe

Darren White

Barry Skelton

Malcolm Gill

Dave Smith

Dale Turrell

Keith Ralphs

Colin Andrews

Bill Sullivan

Carol Ann Slater

Howard Brown

Chaz Walker

Phillip Crossland

Valerie Redmond

Basil Lewis

Terry Carrott

Eric Smith

Roger Hateley

Neville Atkinson

Brian Mellonby

Bob Brown

Bob and Mary Bayes

William Fussey

Jim Bloom

Ruth Waites

Mike Wilson

David Wilcockson

Alex Schofield

Appendix A

Britain's worst train disasters

Here is a list of railway disasters of Britain in the order of death toll. I have numbered them and listed those with the same death toll in order of date. As you can see, Lockington is the 79th worst rail disaster, the worst being a troop train during the First World War colliding with an oncoming train and bursting into flames.

No	Date	Location	Death Toll
1	22 May 1915	Quintinshill, Scotland	227
2	12 October 1952	Harrow and Wealdstone	112
3	4 December 1957	Lewisham	90
4	12 June 1889	Armagh	78
5	28 December 1879	Tay Bridge, Scotland	75
6	5 November 1967	Hither Green	49
7	28 February 1975	Moorgate (London Underground)	43
8	30 September 1945	Bourne End	43
9	12 December 1988	Clapham Junction	35
10	10 December 1937	Castlecary	35
11	24 December 1874	Shipton-on-Cherwell	34

No	Date	Location	Death Toll
12	20 August 1868	Abergele	33
13	24 October 1868	South Croydon	32
14	5 October 1999	Ladbroke Grove	31
15	26 October 1947	Goswick	28
16	30 June 1906	Salisbury	28
17	4 November 1940	Norton Fitzwarren	27
18	27 June 1928	Darlington	25
19	16 September 1887	Hexthorpe	25
20	10 September 1874	Norwich Thorpe	25
21	17 April 1948	Winsford	24
22	16 July 1884	Penistone (Bullhouse Bridge)	24
23	30 December 1941	Eccles	23
24	25 August 1861	Clayton Tunnel	23
25	28 December 1906	Elliot Junction	22
26	1 January 1946	Lichfield	20
27	10 July 1905	Hall Road, Liverpool	20
28	18 December 1915	St Bedes Junction, Jarrow	19
29	26 December 1962	Coppenall Junction	18
30	15 October 1907	Shrewsbury	18
31	20 June 1870	Newark	18
32	23 January 1955	Sutton Coldfield	17
33	26 January 1921	Abermule	17
34	27 July 1903	Glasgow St Enoch	16
35	27 January 1874	Bo'ness Junction	16
36	2 September 1861	Kentish Town	16
37	21 September 1951	Weedon	15
38	13 October 1928	Charfield, Gloucestershire	15
391	7 September 1912	Ditton Junction	15
40	7 August 1876	Radstock, Somerset	15
41	12 December 1870	Stairfoot	15
42	13 October 1862	Winchburgh	15
43	16 March 1951	Doncaster	14

No	Date	Location	Death Toll
44	15 June 1935	Welwyn Garden City	14
45	3 November 1924	Lytham	14
46	1 September 1913	Ais Gill	14
47	19 September 1906	Grantham	14
48	22 December 1894	Chelford	14
49	21 January 1876	Abbots Ripton	14
50	23 August 1858	Round Oak	14
51	30 July 1984	Polmont	13
52	2 December 1955	Barnes	13
53	24 August 1927	Sevenoaks	13
54	12 August 1893	Llantrisant	13
55	2 August 1873	Wigan	13
56	7 June 1865	Rednal	13
57	6 July 1978	Taunton	12
58	8 April 1953	Stratford, London	12
59	28 September 1934	Winwick Junction	12
60	14 February 1927	Hull	12
61	24 December 1910	Hawes Junction	12
62	2 October 1872	Kirtlebridge	12
63	6 January 1968	Hixon	11
64	20 November 1955	Milton	11
65	23 January 1911	Pontypridd	11
66	1 September 1905	Witham	11
67	11 June 1897	Welshampton	11
68	7 June 1865	Rednal	11
69	28 February 2001	Great Heck, Selby	10
70	20 December 1973	Ealing	10
71	30 January 1958	Dagenham East	10
72	15 August 1953	Irk Valley Junction	10
73	2 April 1937	Battersea Park	10
74	24 September 1917	Bere Ferrers, Devon	10
75	14 August 1915	Weedon	10

No	Date	Location	Death Toll
76	1 January 1915	Ilford	10
77	11 November 1890	Norton Fitzwarren	10
78	9 June 1865	Staplehurst	10
79	26 July 1986	Lockington	9
80	28 February 1967	Stechford	9
81	24 December 1841	Sonning Cutting	9
82	2 November 1892	Thirsk	8
83	11 August 1880	Wennington Junction	8
84	26 December 1870	Hatfield	8
85	6 November 2004	Ufton Nervet	7
86	10 May 2002	Potters Bar	7
87	16 April 1979	Paisley	7
88	31 July 1967	Thirsk	7
89	16 July 1961	Singleton Bank	7
90	19 January 1918	Little Salkend	7
91	29 January 1910	Stoats Nest (now Coulsdon North)	7
92	2 September 1898	Wellingborough	7
93	26 November 1870	Harrow	7
94	20 February 1860	Tottenham	7
95	19 September 1997	Southall	6
96	6 June 1975	Nuneaton	6
97	11 June 1972	Eltham Well Hall	6
98	7 May 1969	Morpeth	6
99	5 May 1953	Ystrad Caron level crossing	6
100	4 March 1853	Dixon Fold	6
101	10 May 1848	Shrivenham	6

This list does not include any road transport disasters that have occurred due to a train collision. In 1947 an army truck carrying German prisoners of war was struck by a train at the level crossing at Burton Agnes just five miles from Bridlington. Twelve people were killed, all of whom were on the truck.

Appendix B

Train accidents at level crossings 1986-2008

Year	Number	Year	Number
1986	63	1998	41
1987	58	1999	31
1988	61	2000	33
1989	51	2001	22
1990	41	2002	21
1991	40	2003	63
1992	47	2004	58
1993	39	2005	61
1994	30	2006	51
1995	26	2007	41
1996	39	2008	40
1997	30		

Appendix C

Train accident fatalities at level crossings 1986-2008

Year	Passengers	Rail Employees	Other Vehicle Occupants	Total
1986	8	0	13	21
1987	0	0	6	6
1988	0	0	6	6
1989	1	0	6	7
1990	0	1	3	4
1991	0	0	5	5
1992	0	0	7	7
1993	0	0	3	3
1994	0	0	5	5
1995	0	0	3	3
1996	0	0	3	3
1997	0	0	0	0
1998	0	0	4	4
1999	0	0	3	3
2000	0	0	3	3
2001	0	0	2	2
2002	0	0	2	2
2003	0	1	8	9
2004	5	1	4	10
2005	0	1	6	7
2006	0	0	0	0
2007	0	0	3	3
2008	0	0	2	2

Note the high death toll in 1986 and 2004 for passengers.
This is due to the crashes at Lockington and Ufton Nervet.

Appendix D

Lockington crash vehicles statistics

Train details	Carriage 1	Carriage 2	Carriage 3	Carriage 4
Official Number	54434	51278	53016	54034
Type	Driving trailer composite	Driving motor brake second	Driving motor brake second	Driving trailer composite
DMU Class	105	105	114	114
Length	17.5m	17.5m	19.5m	19.5m
Weight	24.5 tonnes	31.5 tonnes	39.7 tonnes	30.6 tonnes

Van details	Van
Registration plate	GWX 475T
Make	Ford
Colour	Blue
Model	Escort 45 1300
Engine size	1298
Year	1979
Fuel	Petrol
Mileage	62,684
Seating	Driver and passenger seat front only

DEDICATED TO THE MEMORY
OF

GREGORY ADDISON
WAYNE HARMAN
HELEN LODGE
ELSIE MARSTERS
HERBERT MARSTERS
CHRISTINE QUINN
ANNETTE STORK
WAYNE TELLING
JOAN WILSON

WHO DIED 26TH JULY 1986
IN THE LOCKINGTON RAIL CRASH

AND IN RECOGNITION
OF THE BRAVERY
OF THE EMERGENCY SERVICES
WHO ATTENDED

Memorial in winter.

Printed in Great Britain
by Amazon

19535806R00139